Ethics and Military Practice

International Studies on Military Ethics

THE SERIES IS EDITED UNDER THE AUSPICES OF
THE INTERNATIONAL SOCIETY FOR MILITARY
ETHICS IN EUROPE (EUROISME)

Editor-in-Chief

Ted van Baarda (The Netherlands)

Editorial Board

Jovan Babić (*University of Belgrade, Serbia*)
Per Bauhn (*Linnæus University, Sweden*)
Jean-François Caron (*Nazarbayev University,
Kazakhstan and University of Opole, Poland*)
Bruno Coppieters (*Free University Brussels, Belgium*)
Thomas R. Elssner (*Bishopric of the German Armed Forces, Germany*)
Eric Germain (*Ministry of Defence, France*)
Edwin R. Micewski (*National Defence Academy, retired, Austria/USA*)
Patrick Mileham (*Council of Military Education Committees
of United Kingdom Universities, United Kingdom*)

VOLUME 9

The titles published in this series are listed at *brill.com/isme*

Ethics and Military Practice

Edited by

Désirée Verweij, Peter Olsthoorn and Eva van Baarle

BRILL
NIJHOFF

LEIDEN | BOSTON

Cover illustration: Dutch soldiers training near the river Hollands Diep. Copyright Mediacentrum Defensie. Originally published in Dutch as *Ethiek en de militaire praktijk*, Boom, The Hague, 2020. Translation: Kees Offringa.

Library of Congress Cataloging-in-Publication Data

Names: Verweij, Désirée, editor. | Olsthoorn, Peter, editor. |
    Baarle, Eva van, editor.
Title: Ethics and military practice / edited by Désirée Verweij,
    Peter Olsthoorn, and Eva van Baarle.
Description: Leiden ; Boston : Brill Nijhoff, [2022] | Series: International
    studies on military ethics, 2214-7926 ; vol. 9 | Includes index.
Identifiers: LCCN 2022006165 (print) | LCCN 2022006166 (ebook) |
    ISBN 9789004512467 (hardback) | ISBN 9789004512474 (ebook)
Subjects: LCSH: Military ethics. | War–Moral and ethical aspects.
Classification: LCC U22 .E84 2022 (print) | LCC U22 (ebook) |
    DDC 174/.9355–dc23/eng/20220209
LC record available at https://lccn.loc.gov/2022006165
LC ebook record available at https://lccn.loc.gov/2022006166

Typeface for the Latin, Greek, and Cyrillic scripts: "Brill". See and download: brill.com/brill-typeface.

ISSN 2214-7926
ISBN 978-90-04-51246-7 (hardback)
ISBN 978-90-04-51247-4 (e-book)

Copyright 2022 by Koninklijke Brill NV, Leiden, The Netherlands.
Koninklijke Brill NV incorporates the imprints Brill, Brill Nijhoff, Brill Hotei, Brill Schöningh, Brill Fink, Brill mentis, Vandenhoeck & Ruprecht, Böhlau and V&R unipress.
All rights reserved. No part of this publication may be reproduced, translated, stored in a retrieval system, or transmitted in any form or by any means, electronic, mechanical, photocopying, recording or otherwise, without prior written permission from the publisher. Requests for re-use and/or translations must be addressed to Koninklijke Brill NV via brill.com or copyright.com.

This book is printed on acid-free paper and produced in a sustainable manner.

Contents

List of Illustrations   VII
Notes on Contributors   VIII

1   Introduction
    Ethics and Military Practice   1
        Désirée Verweij

2   Fostering Reflective Practice and Moral Competence
    Ethics Education in the Military   15
        Eva van Baarle

3   'The Roof, the Roof, the Roof is on Fire'
    Moral Standards and Moral Disengagement in Military Organisations   24
        Eva van Baarle and Marjon Blom-Terhell

4   Loyalty
    A Grey Virtue?   40
        Peter Olsthoorn and Marjon Blom-Terhell

5   Moral Injury
    The Psychological Impact of Morally Critical Situations   53
        Tine Molendijk

6   Ethics and Technology   67
        Christine Boshuijzen-Van Burken

7   An Organisational Perspective on Military Ethics   83
        Eric-Hans Kramer, Herman Kuipers and Miriam de Graaff

8   Morality
    Foundation for Competent Professionals   100
        G. J. van Doorn

Index   127

Illustrations

Figures

8.1 The ethics pyramid; reflection upon morality: Standards and the underlying values, as foundation for our action   104

8.2 The three-layered Iceberg: operative (upper current), cognitive and affective (under current)   111

8.3 The ethics pyramid and the didactics iceberg: Reflection upon morality and action based on professional attitude   115

8.4 Reflective practitioning at a glance: The continuous circular relationship between ethical reflection and practical action   121

Table

5.1 Current PTSD models and Moral Injury model   58

Notes on Contributors

Eva van Baarle

is assistant professor of Military Ethics and Philosophy at the Netherlands Defence Academy. In 2018, she obtained her doctorate with her research into fostering the moral competence of military personnel through ethics education. She is currently involved in the action research 'Towards a socially safe Defence culture' as project leader. In addition to her work at the Netherlands Defence organisation, she is conducting research in collaboration with the Amsterdam UMC (VUmc department) into the further professionalisation of ethics support in healthcare and into promoting a 'just culture' in healthcare organisations.

Marjon Blom-Terhell

has been employed in the Netherlands Defence organisation at the Royal Netherlands Marechaussee since 2003. In addition to various managerial and staff positions, she has also worked as an assistant professor of military ethics, leadership and human resource management at the Netherlands Defence Academy. She currently serves as Brigade Commander Zeeland West-Brabant.

Christine Boshuijzen-Van Burken

works as a researcher at the University of New South Wales (UNSW) at the Australian Defence Force Academy (ADFA) in Canberra, Australia. She holds degrees in Human Kinetic Engineering (BSC), Mechanical Engineering (BSC) and Christian Studies of Science and Society (MA). She has held positions at the Netherlands Defence Academy, Delft University of Technology, Eindhoven University of Technology, Erasmus University Rotterdam and Linnaeus University in Sweden. Before starting her doctoral research, she worked in industry. Christine is a reservist in the National Reserve Corps.

G. J. van Doorn

is an academic lecturer on Leadership, Ethics and HRM at the Netherlands Defence Academy (NLDA), and a personal, executive and team coach *on call* for the Expertise Centre for Defense Management (ECLD). His research focuses on the ontological and epistemological foundations of coaching as 'the new leadership', including its implications for practitioners.

NOTES ON CONTRIBUTORS

Miriam de Graaff

is a psychologist and communication scientist. She obtained a doctorate at the University of Twente for studying moral dilemmas and decision-making in complex situations. She currently works as head of the Centre of Expertise for Communication & Engagement within the Royal Netherlands Armed Forces, and has her own organisational advice and training agency 'KreOs Leiderschap & Ethiek'. In 2015 she was nominated for the Young Talent Award of the Dutch Women in Leadership election.

Eric-Hans Kramer

is full professor of Military Management and Organisation at the Netherlands Defence Academy. Previously, he was associate professor of Human Factors and System Safety at the same institute. He has conducted various studies into organisational issues in the military and in setting up research and education in the field of psychosocial dynamics for organisations acting as instruments of force.

Herman Kuipers

is emeritus professor of Sociotechnical organizational analysis at Eindhoven University of Technology and emeritus professor of Organisational Psychology at the Royal Military Academy in Breda. After his retirement he was active as an independent consultant and researcher at Bos & Kuipers. In his work for the foundation Promotum Promovendi he was involved in assisting external doctoral students.

Tine Molendijk

is a cultural anthropologist with a cross-disciplinary orientation, specialised in the themes of violence, military culture and mental health, particularly post-traumatic stress disorder and moral injury. In 2020 she obtained a doctorate at Radboud University with her research into the role of political practices and public perceptions in moral injury among Srebrenica and Afghanistan veterans. She is currently an assistant professor at the Netherlands Defence Academy, and heads an NWO NWA research project focused on contextual aspects of moral injury among both military and police personnel.

Peter Olsthoorn

is associate professor of Military Leadership and Ethics at the Netherlands Defence Academy. He lectures in the fields of ethics, public administration, leadership and media. In addition, he teaches Human Rights and Ethics in the

Frontex master programme. So far, his research has focused on military ethics, leadership, drones and border control.

Désirée Verweij
is professor of Philosophy and Ethics at the Netherlands Defence Academy and at the Centre for International Conflict Analysis and Management (CICAM) at Radboud University Nijmegen. Her research concerns both fundamental and applied ethics and includes themes associated with both the individual level and the socio-political level of military ethics. These themes include 'moral judgment', 'responsibility', 'recognition', 'human rights', and the 'tradition of just war'.

CHAPTER 1

Introduction

Ethics and Military Practice

Désirée Verweij

1 Ethics and Military Ethics

Should I give the order to fire? Or maybe not? Is there a risk of too many civilian casualties? What should I do? And what will happen if I wait too long before deciding? (...) Should I confront my colleagues with their disrespectful attitude towards the local population? Or will that make me look overly politically correct and will they thus stop listening to me altogether? (...) Why can't I help this sick and malnourished child? We have sufficient medication in our compound, and if we don't help the child it will probably die. (...) How do I convince these Afghan policemen in training that it is not a good idea to lock up female detainees in an ammunition depot when there are no separate cells for women? (...) Isn't it strange that we first destroy half a village and then pay for the damage suffered by civilians? (...) What exactly are we doing here?'

These are just some of the many moral questions that soldiers are faced with today. Questions that are by no means simple. In order to answer such questions adequately, it is essential to first have a sound understanding of what exactly moral questions and dilemmas are. For this we must know what ethics is and what military ethics as a form of applied ethics implies. This introductory chapter discusses the key concepts from military ethics and thus lays the foundation for the following chapters. First, in section 2, the concepts of ethics and military ethics are described in more detail and the three levels that can be distinguished in military ethics are discussed. This section will demonstrate that the basis for critical reflection (for that is what ethics is) lies at the micro (i.e. individual) level. For this reason, the individual as 'moral agent' is addressed in detail in section 3. We will look at the individual as a being capable of exercising moral judgment and of acting on the basis of the approval or disapproval inherent in that judgment. The socially responsible behaviour expected from the individual members of a community originates from the recognition of oneself and others as moral agents. This recognition

---

© KONINKLIJKE BRILL NV, LEIDEN, 2022 | DOI:10.1163/9789004512474_002

thus constitutes the moral point of view and in that sense it is of crucial importance, also in military practice. Section 4 therefore elaborates on the concept of 'recognition' as described by the contemporary German philosopher Axel Honneth, who has discussed the relevance of this concept to ethics at length and uses a threefold division that corresponds to the aforementioned threefold division in military ethics. Again with the help of Honneth, Section 5 goes on to demonstrate that, and how, recognition of the other may turn into disregard, causing the morally responsible point of view to disappear. This risk is inherent in military practice, where binary 'friend-foe thinking' often seems to prevail and sometimes seems to be encouraged. However, this does not change the fact that soldiers are also expected to act in a morally responsible way, which is not only a requirement imposed on soldiers by contemporary democratic societies, but also a requirement that traditionally takes centre stage in the Just War Tradition (JWT). Section 6 therefore explains that and how the criterion of 'right intention' as developed in the JWT represents the moral point of view – and thus the recognition of the other. The final section (7) describes how this recognition of the other based on the 'right intention' shapes one's responsibility towards the other, also, and particularly, in military practice. This shows that morally responsible action not only extends beyond the self in the sense that it takes the values and associated interests of the other into consideration, but that it does so too in the sense that it takes account of the context in which the encounter with the other takes place and attaches the right weight to those contextual factors. That this is far from easy, especially in the complex conditions that characterise military practice, will be illustrated and elaborated on from different perspectives in the following chapters of this book. Section 7 concludes with an overview of the different ways in which this is done. This introductory chapter, by discussing a number of the key concepts, thus lays the foundation for the subsequent chapters.

2   Ethics and Military Ethics at Three Levels

Ethics can be defined as critical reflection on morality, and morality as the set of moral standards and values of a particular community in a given period. The latter means that morality and therefore also moral standards and values are closely linked to the historical and socio-cultural context in which a person lives. Morality is therefore relative, in the sense that moral standards and values are bound by time and place. However, this does not mean that it does not matter whether and how a person makes a moral judgment, certainly not within the context in which this moral judgment is made, or sometimes, to everyone's surprise, is *not* made. Because of the very diversity of moral standards and values, critical reflection on morality is relevant. Critical reflection, in accordance with the original meaning of the Greek concept of '*krinein*', signifies the ability to judge adequately. Notably, an adequate judgment is a well-considered judgment and therefore not a preconception, since a preconception is literally a premature judgment, which has not yet been subjected to reflection and to that extent is not adequate. Critical reflection on morality is, as indicated, aimed at the moral standards and values shaping a specific practice. In that sense, a standard refers to a rule which is – or should be – based on an underlying value. If it is not, this rule is literally and figuratively valueless or worthless; for the underlying value, which is or should be the determining factor, is absent or is not perceived as such. The rule thus appears to have no value, and following a rule that has no value is pointless; for a value is an inner conviction or a principle; it is something perceived as important, and the more importance a person attaches to a value or a principle, the more it will determine that person's behaviour. It is thus self-evident that 'valueless' rules have little guiding power. This can also be seen clearly in military practice. Values that almost every soldier finds important are 'comradeship' and 'loyalty' (see Chapter 4). These values are often felt so strongly that having a rule based on those values would seem entirely superfluous. Yet not all soldiers attach the same value to comradeship and loyalty. This is because the way people perceive the importance of values is a personal matter, and therefore not the same for everyone. This is exactly why to some people ethics is entirely meaningless and few values are considered really important (this will be discussed in more detail below). The general definition of ethics makes clear that ethics is not the same as rules and that conflicts about values demonstrate that it is not always possible to make a clear distinction between 'right' and 'wrong', only increasing the need to be able to make adequate judgments (see Chapter 2).

In relation to military ethics, three levels can be broadly distinguished: the individual level, the organisational level and the socio-political level. These three levels determine the focus of the critical reflection. A military professional works in or on behalf of a certain organisation, frequently together with others and with specific – often technologically sophisticated – material (cf. Chapter 6). A military organisation is structured in a specific way and the work is also organised in a specific way (see Chapter 7). In addition, every organisation has a specific culture, which in this context means that things are seen in a certain way and that people behave in a certain way. However, the organisation is not isolated from its environment; it is embedded in a socio-political context. The Defence organisation, and particularly the armed forces, is a government organisation with specific tasks related to the monopoly of force vested in the armed forces. In a democratic society, this means in concrete terms that society has mandated the armed forces to use force in its name if this is necessary to protect national and international security (the rule of law) and the associated values and interests. The performance of these tasks requires due care and responsible conduct based on this mandate. The global division into three levels of military ethics forms a distinction, not a partition. That is to say that the levels are often directly linked to one another, and many moral/ethical questions and dilemmas affect more than one level. Notably, the basis for the critical reflection being done at the various levels lies at the individual (or: micro) level.

3 The Human Being as Moral Agent

Every individual soldier is – just like every other person – the protagonist in his or her own narrative. This personal story makes him/her the person that he/she is. That does not mean that it completely determines what or who he/she can become, but any change, and therefore any formation, must begin with a person's own individual story and the values playing a role in it (see Chapter 8). People are moral agents and the values they have and pursue as moral beings determine the choices they make. The values guiding a person's narrative are linked to the socio-cultural environment in which that person grows up. This environment is determined by a number of basic principles and beliefs (values) regarding the way people interact with each other and carry out their daily activities. The combination of the values from a person's narrative and the values provided by his/her socio-cultural environment also influence the way in which people educate children and young adults and mould their character. A child growing up may be taught, for example, to deal with other people with respect and to be modest or, conversely, to be bold and stand up for himself, to be diligent and hardworking, or to focus on having fun and doing exciting new things. In some children curiosity is stimulated, in others it is discouraged. It is also possible that a child or young adult is hardly told or taught anything, and has to figure things out for himself, forced to learn solely from his mistakes. So it makes quite a difference where one is born, and by whom one is raised and formed. One's environment largely determines which values one does or does not consider important. This does not alter the fact that the values that people have grown up with since childhood may differ greatly from one another, even within a specific social context or culture. Moreover, people are often not really aware of their own beliefs and principles (values), nor of the fact that these values are decisive for the steps they take or do not take in their lives, and the things they do or refrain from doing. Education and formation take place not only within the family, but also outside it, particularly in school. Thus also in military training institutes, in which education also implies a transferral of norms and values to future soldiers. For educators and trainers it is important to know that values are strongly linked to feelings and emotions, as argued by the ancient Greek philosopher Aristotle and demonstrated by contemporary socio-psychological and neuroscientific research (cf., for example, Den Boer 2003, Churchland 1986, Damasio 1994 and 2003, Haidt 2001 and 2004 and Malabou 2004). That insight is crucial if ethics is understood as critical reflection on morality, and therefore also when dealing with formation (see also Chapter 8). Because if a person's social emotions are not developed, or hardly so, then that person's sense of values – both their own and those of others – will likewise be undeveloped or underdeveloped (cf., for example, Damasio 2003). The concepts of ethics, morality, values and moral standards are then without meaning; a person will know – at best – that the violation of certain rules may have consequences, but he/she does not experience or sense the importance of the values underlying the rules. Also, and particularly, in military practice, this may have far-reaching consequences if rules are not sufficient – and the problem is that they never entirely are. There can never be sufficient rules to cover the infinite variety of situations that may occur in complex practical circumstances. This means that the soldier in question will have to think for himself or herself how to act responsibly, however, this gets tricky if a person does not realise that certain values are at stake or at risk of being violated (this is discussed in more detail in Chapter 3 using the concept of moral disengagement). In that case, such moral blindness or moral short-sightedness will soon lead to problems for all parties involved, including the soldier himself or herself and the organisation he or she works for. After all, the fact that one person fails to see certain values does not mean that others fail to do so as well. (Chapter 5 addresses the 'moral injury' that soldiers may suffer in this type of situation.) The very fact that values are so decisive for choices and actions, and those choices and actions may have far-reaching consequences in complex contexts, makes it important for us to learn to reflect critically on our own values and on those of others. That means that we learn to identify the moral agent in ourselves and in others and become able to enter into a dialogue from a moral-ethical perspective. Recognising yourself and others as moral agents is therefore a *conditio sine qua non* for socially responsible behaviour. In other words, there can be no socially responsible behaviour without such recognition.

4 Recognising the Other as the Moral Point of View

The importance of recognising the other has been described extensively by the German philosopher Axel Honneth, for the first time in his ground-breaking work *Kampf um Anerkennung* (1992), which was translated into English three years later as *The Struggle for Recognition: The Moral Grammar of Social Conflicts*. In line with the insights of several philosophers, psychologists and psychoanalysts, Honneth also argues that individuals learn to shape their identities in and through relationships of mutual recognition. Those relationships with others are crucial for further developing one's own identity. Honneth distinguishes three formative relationships of recognition. The first and most basic relationship is the love relationship. This most basic form of intersubjective recognition, which is crucial for developing self-confidence, includes first of all the parent-child relationship, but also friendships and sexual relationships. The second form of intersubjective recognition concerns legal relations and rights. This may include, for example, relationships between citizen and government, employee and company, or tenant and landlord. These relations enable people to manifest themselves as autonomous individuals, and are therefore very important for their sense of self-respect. The third form of intersubjective recognition refers to relationships of solidarity, which means that people express their appreciation for each other's practices and lifestyles. This third form of recognition is crucial for the development of self-esteem. According to Honneth, solidarity is based on appreciating the actions and conduct of others that contribute to achieving a common goal (Honneth in Iorio 2013, p. 250). These three forms of recognition jointly determine a person's moral point of view and enable the development of self-confidence, self-respect and self-esteem respectively, which is crucial for the development of a person's identity. The absence of these relationships of recognition therefore has far-reaching consequences for the development of an individual's identity. This may initially apply to a child which is deprived of the relationship of mutual recognition with the parent and suffers psychological damage as a result, as is shown by many psychological theories. But it may also apply to an adult who experiences a lack of social appreciation caused by, for example, unemployment, poorly paid work or a lack of cultural prestige (cf. also Chapter 5, which explains how the absence of recognition may cause 'moral injury'). People are to a significant degree dependent on recognition by others. Not only in the family context, but also in educational institutes and government organisations. In these 'institutions' people have – and are entitled to have – certain expectations of each other. These 'mutual recognition claims' (Honneth in Petherbridge 2011, p. 392) are decisive for respectful behaviour.

INTRODUCTION

This means that if there is no recognition, respect will be absent as well. Honneth (2014) emphasises that the three forms of recognition mentioned, which together determine the moral point of view, imply a permanent tension (Honneth 2014). In my opinion, this tension is necessary, particularly in military practice. It is therefore better to acknowledge this tension than to reduce it to a binary thinking process, as will be discussed in the next section.

5   Reification: The Failure to Recognise the Other and the Moral Point of View

In the spring of 2005, Honneth was invited to give the 'Tanner Lectures' at the University of California, Berkeley. He chose the subject of 'reification' or, as the original concept is called in German, '*Verdinglichung*'. Honneth uses this concept to explicitly describe the circumstances under which forms of interpersonal recognition can be undermined. Reification occurs when individuals lose sight of their original recognition of each other as persons. In its philosophical context the concept of reification must be placed against the background of the social-cultural criticism in the first three decades of the twentieth century. The term was introduced by Georg Lukács in 1925 and adopted by the *Frankfurter Schule*, in particular by Theodor Adorno. In his Tanner Lectures, Honneth takes Lukács' elaboration of the concept of reification as a starting point. Based on Lukács' text, in which he juxtaposes the 'reifying' attitude with an attitude of empathy and existential engagement, Honneth makes a connection with Heidegger's concept of care (*Sorge*) and John Dewey's concept of practical involvement. Honneth sees these concepts as the most elementary form of recognition in which the importance of the values presented by one's environment is experienced (Honneth 2008, p. 37). The process of reification, on the other hand, is one in which the human perspective of sincere involvement – and with that the moral perspective – is neutralised and eliminated. This perspective is thus transformed into a purely objectifying way of thinking (idem, p. 54). This reductionism causes individuals to deny the elementary recognition they originally experienced in relation to other individuals. This happens particularly in situations where the concrete qualities of individuals are made abstract. The abstract schemes of thought that are formed in this way may lead to selective interpretation, giving rise to and reinforcing preconceptions and stereotypes. When an individual is transformed into a 'thing', exactly those personal qualities that make an individual a fellow human being are lost. Reification therefore means that a person is not (or no longer) able to see those qualities that make individuals human beings (idem p. 148). Honneth discusses various practices that lead to reifying behaviour. The pattern is always the same, it shows a one-sided focus on the achievement of an absolute goal leading to the breaking of all original relationships with the surrounding world and thus to a disengagement of social connections. One of the practices Honneth mentions explicitly is warfare, where the goal of eliminating 'the enemy' becomes an end in itself, to the extent that the recognition of human qualities in everyone qualifying as an 'enemy' disappears. If this abstraction is sufficiently strong, a black-and-white mindset develops in which everyone belonging to a particular community, including non-combatants, is seen as an object to be eliminated.

5.1 Reification in Military Practice: The 'Enemy' in Capital Letters

This way of binary thinking may also give rise to a belief that the military objective is served by manipulating and mistreating the 'enemy', even if non-combatants are concerned, as the excesses in Abu Ghraib prison in Iraq have shown (see Chapters 2, 4 and 7 on Abu Ghraib). This destructive attitude towards an enemy in capital letters has been discussed by several authors in the past, starting with Plato, who in Book V of the *Republic* discusses the way in which a just state wages war. The attitude of soldiers towards their enemies is also addressed in this context. Plato distinguishes between an enemy who may be destroyed and an enemy with whom you will reconcile because you will not wage war with him forever (Plato 1999, V, 470–471). The latter enemy is to be treated as a fellow human being, because he belongs to 'the friendly and kindred' (V, 469–470, p. 265). The other enemy represents 'the foreign'; these enemies were called 'barbarians' by the Greeks (ibidem). Imbued with a considerable sense of self-worth, the ancient Greeks had few qualms about viewing other peoples (i.e. non-Greeks) as barbarians. Failing to fit the Greek standards for being 'civilised' and 'developed', these barbarians were perceived as a threat. The enemy you were allowed to destroy was the enemy who did not belong to your own *polis* or to a similar *polis* and who you did not want anywhere near your *polis* at all. That enemy could be wiped off the face of the earth. Much more can be said about this text and the prototypical binary friend-enemy concept in relation to the present day and in the light of globalisation. But in the context of this introductory chapter, it is important to observe that Plato's main goal in this text is to make clear how a just state wages war and what a just attitude towards the enemy implies. Thus, Plato's text offers a number of building blocks that would be elaborated on later in the course of history by Augustine, the father of the Just War Tradition. In this long-standing tradition, criteria for determining whether a war is just have long been discussed and are still being discussed up to this day. The very existence of this tradition, which

INTRODUCTION

laid the foundations for the Geneva Conventions and international humanitarian law, makes clear that the 'reifying' attitude towards the enemy discussed above is not the only attitude soldiers have, or indeed should have. As said earlier, soldiers are also expected to act in morally responsible way. Far from being new, this premise, which also characterises current debates on military action, has a long history, as evidenced by the Just War Tradition. In particular, the criterion of the 'right intention' developed in this tradition plays a prominent role in these discussions.

6 The 'Right Intention'

In military practice, recognition of the other is also present in the intention from which the 'self' approaches the 'other'. That intention, and with it the recognition which cannot be readily discerned at the outset, only becomes clear and visible in the actions that follow the self's approach of the other. After all, the 'right intention' implies recognition of the individual other as a fellow human being, and with that, of the values of that other and the interests associated with those values. This is why the Just War Tradition also refers to the 'right', or 'just' intention (the term 'just' being derived from the Latin '*iustus*', meaning 'fair'). The concrete meaning and consequence of the above may best be illustrated by using the example of help. Help in a general sense can be provided in a variety of ways and at all of the three levels referred to above (cf. section 2). Help can be provided by an individual, by an organisation and from the (international) political sphere. Help may be, for example, medical, humanitarian or financial in nature, but may also consist of the deployment of military assets – in the form of protection, for instance. The latter notion is central to the Just War Tradition, and that is exactly the reason that the criterion of the right intention plays a key role in this tradition. The right intention prevents the aforementioned reification of the other, also in political and military contexts, and it consequently prevents the deployment of military assets from being based on and leading to 'the love of violence, vengeful cruelty and the lust for power', as Augustine, the spiritual father of the Just War Tradition, characterised the real danger of war (*Contra Faustum*, XXII, 74, in Reichberg et al. 2006). The right intention was traditionally seen as the key to a just war, because only on the basis of the right intention could the other criteria (*ad bellum*, *in bello* and *post bellum*) be adequately met (cf. also Verweij 2019). The right intention refers to that proper inner disposition on the basis of which the intention can be called precisely 'just' (in accordance with the Latin '*iustus*'). As Augustine points out, the right intention, as a key concept and guiding principle within the Just War Tradition, is aimed at countering injustice, in the same way as I counter injustice committed against me by resisting, or injustice committed against others by helping them. The idea behind countering injustice is that doing so will enable people and communities to continue to live in a just and therefore constructive manner. That means that the right (*iustus*) intention also serves as reference point when applying the other principles of the Just War Tradition, which results in proportional actions aimed at achieving peace and security. It is precisely this right intention that entails that non-combatants must be spared. The original concept of the Just War Tradition was developed in recognition of the importance of the connection between three political aims: 'legitimate order', 'justice' and 'peace'. These aims are interdependent, as stated by Augustine in *Contra Faustum* (XXII, 75) in his description of the '*tranquillitas ordinis*' as the peace or social tranquillity that is safeguarded by sound (*iustus*) political policy (cf. also Reichberg 2006, p. 177). The use of military means served these aims. So if I offer help to the other, in a general sense but also concretely by military means, with the right intention, I am in fact focused on the well-being of the other and I also intend to give the other what he/she needs in order to achieve or return to this state of well-being. It does not mean that I decide what help is needed, but that I tailor my actions to what the other asks of me and what the other needs. Nor does it mean, however, that I follow the wishes of the other blindly, completely setting aside my values and associated interests. I may start a dialogue with the other about how help should be provided, or about the consequences that certain actions may have, but the well-being of the other will always be the starting point.

7   Relationality and Responsibility: The 'Self' and the 'Other' in the Military Context

Recognition of the other on the basis of the right intention shows my responsibility towards the other. Responsibility literally means the ability to give a 'response' (cf. also Verweij 2010). There can only be a response if a question is posed. My responsibility is thus my response to the question of the other, to the appeal made to me. This 'relational' interpretation of responsibility, which is thus inherent to my relationship with the other, my recognition of the other and my right intention towards the other, has been thematised by several philosophers (the most famous of whom are Arendt (1989), Weil (1998), Levinas (2010) and Butler (2004)). These philosophers have demonstrated that the relational perspective, in which I recognise the other and the appeal he/she makes to me, determines my moral responsibility. In that sense, these authors

INTRODUCTION

have shown that the right intention vis-à-vis the other prevents reification as discussed by Honneth. However, matters are not as clear-cut as this, particularly in military practice. When the example of giving help is applied in more concrete terms to the aforementioned three levels of military ethics, the complex nature of military ethics soon becomes apparent. The different levels show that recognition of the other, and consequently my respect for the other, my solidarity with the other and my right intention to provide help (for example, by offering protection by military means), does not necessarily imply that the problems – both the other's and my own – have been solved. Both the other and I live in contexts that also include other individuals and other institutions, who or which may have other values and associated interests. These contexts, i.e. the individuals and institutions surrounding me, also relate in a certain way to the help I give to the other. Within those contexts, for example, my help or protection may be viewed as inappropriate, as unjust, or even as betrayal or as disguised self-interest. These potentially divergent interpretations of my help or protection may give rise not only to irritation but also to rejection and resistance. In addition, the other may become so dependent on my help or protection that I must ask myself how long I want, or will be able, to go on providing that help and protection. Briefly put, the context, and the other individuals and institutions featuring in it, have an impact on my relationship with the other. Although the relationship between the self and the other is the most basic relationship, and the most thematised from a moral/ethical perspective, in everyday reality we are simply not a solitary 'self' standing before an equally solitary 'other', under whose gaze we become a responsible being (cf. Levinas 2010). Although the gaze of the other and the relationship with the other are crucial, and the insights of the 'relationality philosophers' are highly relevant, the context within which moral beings encounter each other and together shape the world surrounding them also plays a crucial role. Morally responsible action therefore not only extends beyond the self in the sense that it takes the values and associated interests of the other into consideration, it also encompasses the context in which the encounter with the other occurs and attaches the right (*iustus*) weight to those contextual factors.

This form of morally responsible action will be elaborated on in many different ways in the various chapters of this book. The complexity of military practice, and consequently that of ethics in military practice, is described in more palpable terms. The authors will illustrate the key concepts discussed above from different perspectives and by means of specific case histories, painting a clear picture of the situations and choices that soldiers are faced with. It will also become clear that those choices are by no means easy and demand a great deal from both soldiers and the organisation as a whole.

In Chapter 2, Van Baarle starts with a specific moral dilemma that is analysed from various ethical perspectives, thus showing how this type of analysis may contribute to the development of the moral competence of soldiers. That this is quite necessary is evident from Chapter 3, which uses a recent case to demonstrate how easily moral disengagement occurs and how difficult it may be to identify and combat this phenomenon, both for individual soldiers and for the organisation as a whole. Van Baarle and Blom-Terhell argue that in such situations where standards become blurred a 'just culture' approach offers better perspectives than merely looking for a culprit. After all, identifying a scapegoat will seldom solve the underlying problem. This has everything to do with that typical military virtue, loyalty, which is the main subject of Chapter 4. In this chapter Olsthoorn and Blom-Terhell show that there are two different forms of loyalty (loyalty to the group and loyalty to a principle or profession) and they ask the question how loyal it really is to expect loyalty from your colleagues. The dilemmas discussed in the first four chapters already reveal to some extent the enormous impact that a confrontation with serious moral dilemmas can have on a soldier. This is discussed in more depth by Molendijk in Chapter 5. Using the stories of two service members, she shows that 'moral injury' is a problem that must be taken seriously in military practice. She discusses the distinction between moral injury and PTSD (Post-Traumatic Stress Disorder) and demonstrates that this is not just a clinical and thus mainly individual problem, but that the organisation, society and politics also play a role. Chapter 6 focuses on the relationship between ethics and technology in contemporary military missions. In her discussion of a friendly-fire incident, Boshuijzen-Van Burken shows how moral decision-making is influenced by technology and how technology is embedded in the normative structure of military practice. Technologies are not 'neutral' as is often assumed and may cause clashes between the various moral standards, rules and principles – referred to as 'structure' by Boshuijzen-Van Burken – that characterise military practice. The structure of organisations is also the central theme of Chapter 7, in which Kramer et al. pose the question of how the design of organisations – also referred to as structure or architecture – influences moral responsibility. On the basis of socio-technical business theory, Kramer et al. make a distinction between 'the bureaucratic regime' and 'the flexible regime' and show that these two extremes have a different impact on the way soldiers can deal with the tension between obedience and the autonomous power of judgment. The two regimes therefore have a different impact on moral responsibility. The power of judgment, and latitude to act on the basis of this judgment, are essential preconditions for morally responsible behaviour, and it is the architecture of the organisation that creates the conditions for this. However, having the

INTRODUCTION

right architecture does not mean that the moral responsibility of moral agents is guaranteed, which once again underlines the importance of adequate training and formation of military professionals. This type of training and formation is the main topic of Chapter 8, in which Van Doorn uses seven short case examples to discuss the integration of ethics and didactics. He demonstrates that the reflection on moral standards and values (as illustrated by the metaphor of 'the ethics pyramid') follows the same layered structure as action motivated by emotions and reasoning according to McClelland's 'iceberg model' (the competence concept). Van Doorn describes competent professionals as 'reflective practitioners' and demonstrates that 'reflective practitioning' implies the ability to ask yourself ('reflective') which values and moral standards form the foundation of your own behaviour and that of others, and then translate these into new, self-aware and responsible action in daily practice ('practitioning').

Literature

Arendt, H. (1989). *The Human Condition*. Chicago/Londen: University of Chicago Press.

Boer, J.A. den (2003). *Neurofilosofie. Hersenen, bewustzijn, vrije wil.* Amsterdam: Boom Psychiatrie & Filosofie.

Butler, J. (2004). *Precarious Life: The Powers of Mourning and Violence.* London/ New York: Verso.

Churchland, P.S. (1986). *Neurophilosophy. Toward a Unified Science of the Mind/Brain.* Cambridge, MA: MIT Press.

Damasio, A. (1994). *Descartes' Error: Emotions, Reason and the Human Brain.* London: Vintage.

Damasio, A. (2003). *Het gelijk van Spinoza. Vreugde, verdriet en het voelende brein.* Amsterdam: Wereldbibliotheek. Translation of (2003) *Looking for Spinoza. Joy, Sorrow and the Feeling Brain.* Portsmouth, New Hampshire: Heinemann.

Haidt, J. (2001). 'The Emotional Dog and Its Rational Tail: A Social Intuitionist Approach to Moral Judgment'. *Psychological Review, vol. 108,* no. 4, 814–834.

Haidt, J. and Joseph, C. (2004). 'Intuitive Ethics: How Innate Prepared Intuitions Generate Culturally Variable Virtues'. *Daedalus, Fall 2004,* 133, 4; *ProQuest Central,* 55–67.

Honneth, A. (1995). *The Struggle for Recognition. The Moral Grammar of Social Conflicts.* Cambridge: Polity Press. Translation of (1992) *Kampf um Anerkennung.* Frankfurt am Main: Suhrkamp Verlag.

Honneth, A. (2008). *Reification. A New Look at an Old Idea.* Oxford: Oxford University Press, edited by M. Jay with contributions from Judith Butler, Raymond Geuss and Jonathan Lear (part of the series: The Berkeley Tanner lectures).

Honneth, A. (2014). *Freedom's Right: The Social Foundation of Democratic Life.* Cambridge: Polity Press.

Iorio, G. and Campello, F. (2013). 'Love, Society and Agape: An Interview with Axel Honneth'. *European Journal of Social Theory 16*(2), 246–258; DOI: 10.1177/1368431012459697 est.sagepub.com.

Levinas, E. (2010). *Totaliteit en Oneindigheid. Essay over exterioriteit.* Amsterdam: Boom Filosofie.

Malabou, C. (2004). *Que Faire de Notre Cerveau?* Parijs: Bayard.

Petherbridge, D. (2011). *Axel Honneth: Critical Essays. With a Reply by Axel Honneth.* Brill, DOI 10.1163/ej.9789004208858.i-439.

Plato (1999). *Verzameld werk.* Kapellen: Uitgeverij Pelckmans.

Reichberg et al. (2006). *The Ethics of War: Classical and Contemporary Readings.* Oxford: Blackwell Publishing.

Verweij, D. (2010). *Geweten onder schot.* Amsterdam: Boom Lemma.

Verweij, D. (2019). 'Over 'caritas' en de belofte van de 'juiste intentie'. Terug naar de wortels van rechtvaardigheid in oorlog'. *Algemeen Nederlands Tijdschrift voor Wijsbegeerte, themanummer Oorlog en Rechtvaardigheid, Vol. III*, no. 1.

Weil, S. (1998). *The Way of Justice as Compassion.* New York/Oxford: Rowman & Littlefield Publishers.

CHAPTER 2

Fostering Reflective Practice and Moral Competence
Ethics Education in the Military

Eva van Baarle

1 Introduction

Military personnel encounter moral dilemmas during deployments and in their working environment at home. Moral dilemmas can be defined as situations in which a choice has to be made between two actions, embodying different values. Dealing with moral dilemmas requires moral competence. There is a growing awareness of the need to address ethics during training in the armed forces and to foster moral competence by means of ethics education. In this chapter a specific notion of 'moral competence' is used, that includes six different elements. The following elements can be considered relevant in fostering moral competence: (1) The awareness of one's own personal values and the values of others; (2) The recognition of the moral dimension of a situation and identify which values are at stake or are at risk of violation; (3) The ability to adequately judge a moral question or dilemma; (4) The ability to communicate this judgment; (5) The willingness and ability to act in accordance with this judgment in a morally responsible manner; and (6) The willingness and ability to be accountable to yourself and to others.

This chapter starts with an example of a moral dilemma sketched by Sergeant Major Yvonne van Nieuwburg in the TV series *Kijken in de ziel* ('Gazing into the soul') (NRT 2017). This example is considered from three ethical perspectives: ethics of consequence, ethics of duty and virtue ethics. Subsequently, the meaning of the concept of moral competence is discussed, as well as how ethics education aims to strengthen the moral competence of military personnel.

2 Case Example

In the Dutch TV series *Kijken in de ziel* ('Gazing into the soul') Sergeant Major Yvonne van Nieuwburg talks about her experiences with moral dilemmas as a military nurse. She also talks about her experiences in Afghanistan. As a

© KONINKLIJKE BRILL NV, LEIDEN, 2022 | DOI:10.1163/9789004512474_003

military nurse, she provided care to her own colleagues (Dutch service members), but was frequently also called upon to help the local population, in pursuit of the aim of winning their hearts and minds. The rationale behind this was to gain the local population's support for the mission, possibly leading them to provide important information to the Dutch troops.

> A report comes in announcing there is a patient at the main gate. Yvonne goes there, together with a military physician and a number of colleagues. At the gate is an Afghan father holding a small baby. With the aid of an interpreter, he tells Yvonne that the baby has been bitten by a snake. The man says: 'Here is my baby, help me.' There are a number of vials with antivenom left. She and the military physician call their seniors: 'What should we do?' The father, with a look of mortal fear in his eyes, comes closer and closer to her. Yvonne takes a step back each time: 'Once you're holding the baby, saying no becomes even more difficult.' The senior medical authority of the area makes clear that the antivenom kept in store should be saved to treat the contingent's own personnel. But Yvonne knows that if they send the father and the baby to the local hospital in Tarin Kowt, the baby will not make it. She is furious; for in that case the child will die.

3 Three Perspectives on a Moral Question

Yvonne's case is reflected upon from three perspectives: ethics of consequence, ethics of duty and virtue ethics.

3.1 *Ethics of Consequence (or Consequentialism or Utilitarianism)*
According to ethics of consequence theories, which course of action is morally best defensible is solely determined by the value of its consequences (Bentham 1789; Robson 1996). 'Best' should be understood here according to the original utilitarian principle of 'the greatest degree of happiness for the greatest number of people'. A morally good action is thus characterised by a good result of that action. If the consequences of one action are better than the consequences of other actions we could have taken, then that is the action we should choose.

The scope of the consequences is also relevant in this perspective on a moral question. For whom should we take the consequences into account? Should we also take the future into account?

Utilitarianism (Robson 1996) is a well-known theory in ethics of consequence by which the consequences of an action can be assessed. Utilitarianism focuses on utility; an action is morally just if it creates the greatest possible preponderance of positive over negative consequences for the largest possible group. Utilitarianism is a common variant of ethics of consequence.

What would be the consequences of admitting the baby? Who would be affected by those consequences? As yet, no colleagues from the Dutch contingent have been bitten by a snake. The possibility that this may still happen before new vials have been flown in cannot be ruled out. In that event, what would be the consequences for colleagues and the organisation, and even at the political level? Even if no colleagues are bitten, it still remains to be seen what the consequences would be for Yvonne if she goes against the decision of the most senior medical authority in the area. Would she be able to account for this action without this having repercussions for her career in the Defence organisation?

From the viewpoint of ethics of consequence, the question of whether the baby should be admitted gives rise to the following considerations: the result could be that you not only save the baby's life, but also gain the trust of the local population. But then you might wonder if from then on the entire village would turn to the military hospital for all medical help and what consequences this would have for the local hospital and the people who work there.

If you choose to admit the baby, it still remains to be seen whether you will manage to save the baby's life. What kind of snake was it? Where was the baby bitten and how long ago? If the baby is admitted but still dies, who is responsible? With regard to gaining the local population's trust, the consequences might well be only negative.

If the baby is not admitted, this will have negative consequences not only for the baby but possibly also for the local population's trust. What if this makes them decide not to share information about the placing of Improvised Explosive Devices (IEDs)? That could possibly cost the lives of Dutch colleagues.

It should also be mentioned that admitting or not admitting the baby may also have negative consequences for Yvonne herself. Will she consider the choice she makes justifiable based on her personal values? How will she view her decision in retrospect?

Consequences of actions lie in the future and are therefore always uncertain. You can try to predict the consequences, but you'll never be entirely sure. Yvonne's case makes it clear that a moral question can also be answered in various ways from the perspective of ethics of consequence.

3.2 Ethics of Duty (or Deontology)

The word 'deontology' is derived from the Greek word for duty *'deon'*. Ethics of duty means that actions are not justified by their consequences, but that the nature of the action should also be considered. This perspective is rooted in the principle of the 'categorical imperative', developed by the German philosopher Immanuel Kant (Kant 1785). The best-known formulation of the categorical imperative is: act as if the maxims of your action were to become a universal law of nature. In other words, would you allow everyone else to act like this? If the answer is yes, then your action is morally correct. It is important to note that this duty also applies if the consequences are detrimental.

A mistake that is easily made in the military context is to interpret the ethics of duty as 'following orders' or *'Befehl ist Befehl'*. It is not about performing every duty indiscriminately but, as indicated above, about following duties that give expression to a universal law (rule) that should be applicable at all times.

The oath taken by nurses is very much akin to such a law: a duty to provide the best possible care to the patient based on the values of humanity and equality. Viewed from the perspective of the oath this is an end in itself, and not a means to win the hearts and minds of the local population. To a nurse or doctor in public healthcare it should not matter whether the father of the baby in the case is an influential village elder, a solitary individual or a member of the Taliban.

Yvonne's dilemma seems rooted rather in the dual use of medical personnel within the Defence organisation than in the existence of dual loyalties (Annas 2008; cf. also Chapter 4). According to George Annas, dual use entails, on the one hand, the moral duty of medical personnel towards their patients and, on the other, deploying medical personnel as effectively as possible. The underlying moral question is whether, and if so under what circumstances, medical personnel may be expected to act contrary to their medical ethics. This could be so in the event of military necessity where military of national security is at stake. Of course, the question is when exactly military necessity can be said to exist. The US military believed military necessity to exist when during the First Gulf War it prescribed the barely tested drug pyridostigmine bromide as protection against nerve gas. The US Food & Drug Administration (FDA) normally monitors the use of this drug very closely, but gave the Pentagon special permission to prescribe the drug at its own discretion (Annas 2008). Based on the principle of military necessity, the question in respect of Yvonne's case could be whether it is justified to save a minimum quantity of medication for medical assistance to one's own personnel, which consequently may not be used when civilians with injuries show up.

3.3 *Virtue Ethics*

One of the oldest ethical perspectives, virtue ethics has been receiving renewed attention in recent years. It aims to offer an alternative to ethical perspectives that give precedence to consequences (ethics of consequence) or universal laws or principles (ethics of duty). The emphasis in virtue ethics lies not on weighing outcomes or following rules but on building moral character. A virtue can be described as a valuable character trait that can be acquired through practice. Virtues are acquired by putting them into practice, they are not innate qualities. Examples of virtues are fairness and justness. What is fair or just may vary according to context, it is about finding the 'golden mean' in each situation. This may be achieved through practice and by reflecting on situations from the past (Aristotle 1999).

In the military context, it is interesting to examine what virtues are important for soldiers. More traditional military virtues such as bravery, loyalty and discipline appear mainly directed towards colleagues and the organisation. As Olsthoorn points out, loyalty, for example, is not so much about loyalty to personal values as about loyalty to the group or organisation (Olsthoorn 2010; cf. also Chapter 4). In Yvonne's case, loyalty seems to be mainly about obedience towards the organisation, or loyalty to (the safety of) her colleagues. It seems to be less about loyalty to the local population or to personal or professional values, such as the well-being of the patient or humanity.

In Yvonne's case, a question derived from virtue ethics could be: what would a good military nurse do in this situation? And which virtues does that involve? These types of questions and answers may help define the role of medical personnel at the Defence organisation. Which virtues should they possess? How do those virtues relate to one another? How do we train medical personnel, or how do we shape their thinking? In the series *Kijken in de ziel*, Yvonne herself says: 'No, I'm there first of all for my colleagues, that's my priority; that's why I'm a nurse (...).' Interestingly, almost at the same time she says: 'Yvonne is sometimes different from the soldier Van Nieuwburg'. How do these two, or perhaps even three, value systems relate to one another? If these value systems clash, to what extent are you able to hold yourself to account?

4 Moral Competence

What would you do in Yvonne's situation? What values are at stake? Moral competence is about recognising the values that are at stake, being able to name them, forming a judgment, and being able to communicate that judgment to others, even if they may not agree with it. Moral competence also implies that you are able to act according to that judgment and to account to others, but also to yourself, about the choices you have made. Moral competence therefore does not only relate to a level of knowledge. Indeed, the idea of 'preparedness to act' indicates that a certain attitude is required. (Karssing 2000; Verweij 2005; Sherblom 2012; Van Baarda et al. 2006; Wortel and Bosch 2011; Van Baarle et al. 2015).

One of the values at stake in the case is the life and well-being of the baby: Yvonne knows that if they do not admit the baby, the baby will not make it. However, the most senior medical authority in the area has decided that the patient may not be admitted. The vials must be kept for the contingent's own personnel. In Yvonne's words: 'As a nurse I think: you know what's going to happen, that child will die, that's the result of that decision.' So for a military nurse there is a clash of values: on the one hand, the loyalty or obedience in respect of the decision of the most senior medical authority in the area, and, on the other, the care for the patient. Care for the baby should be aimed at easing his or her suffering and achieving the best possible quality of life under the circumstances. This is where values related to the military profession and the nursing profession clash. What exactly are the values Yvonne stands for in her work as a military nurse? For whom is she in Afghanistan? Is she first a nurse and only then a soldier, or the other way around?

Of course, besides being a military nurse, Yvonne is also always a human being, with values that are important to her personally. In the TV interview she says: 'As 'Yvonne' I am furious and think: oh, but we've got one or two vials left, haven't we, why not give those then?' So besides values related to the military nursing profession, there are also personal values at play. Yvonne is not alone at the gate; personal values may also play a role for the physician and her military colleagues.

In addition to recognising the moral dimension of situations, moral competence also involves a number of other elements, such as the ability to judge a moral question or dilemma and to communicate this judgment. Such communication is particularly difficult when not everyone agrees with each other. Yvonne is at the gate with a military physician and a number of other colleagues. One may be thinking mainly of the consequences for colleagues, while the other considers the medical oath to be of paramount importance. For moral competence, besides forming a judgment and communicating this judgment, it is important to be willing and able to act in accordance with the judgment and to be able to be accountable to yourself and to others.

In Yvonne's case, how do you arrive at a responsible moral judgment? Practice shows that some colleagues judging a military question will often do so from a single specific perspective, that of ethics of consequence, for example. Other colleagues will sometimes judge and argue from an entirely different perspective, for example one that is mainly concerned with duties. In the practice of ethics education, it sometimes seems as if people are talking at cross-purposes. The trick is to look at a moral question from different perspectives in order to arrive at a well-considered judgment.

5 Principles for Ethics Education for Soldiers

Ethics education at the Netherlands Defence organisation is aimed at fostering the moral competence of military personnel. For ethics education, three potential theoretical points of departure are relevant. Firstly, virtue ethics, aimed at developing personal values and identity. Moral considerations begin with the individual, the moral agent. The formation of this moral agent is therefore of great importance (as also noted in Chapter 1 and Chapter 7). Secondly, the Socratic, dialogic attitude. And lastly, 'live learning', as a method of reflection on (one's own) practical experiences (Van Baarle 2018). These three points of departure are discussed in more detail below.

As indicated earlier, moral competence begins with recognition of the moral dimension of a situation (Wortel & Bosch 2011). In order to recognise the moral dimension of a situation, it is important to recognise which values are at stake. This presupposes that people are already aware of their personal values. Examining personal values is therefore a significant element of ethics education and training. A virtue ethics approach supports such examination of personal values, as this approach revolves around motives, intentions, emotions and desires. During their ethics education, participants reflect on situations in which choices have to be made, and then on their role in those choice processes.

A 'Socratic attitude' (Kessels et al. 2002; Wortel & Verweij 2008) is an important precondition for entering into a dialogue about a moral question or dilemma. It means: being able to listen, deferring judgment and asking in-depth questions, in contrast to entering into a debate where the aim is to convince others. Learning or fostering a Socratic attitude is considered an important element in training moral reflection in ethics education.

A helpful pedagogical method for promoting 'live learning' is Theme-Centred Interaction (TCI) (Cohn 1976; Van de Braak 2011; Van Baarle 2017). Lecturers who use this method endeavour to create a dynamic balance between the four factors that are recognised in each learning or work situation in a group: the task, being the purpose of the course or training or a particular element thereof (it), the group (we), the individual (I), and the context (globe).

This approach ensures that participants are able to link (sometimes abstract) theories to their own practical experiences. This method is thus conducive to fostering participants' moral competence.

6 Conclusion

In the case we discussed, a split-second decision has to be made and there is little time for reflection. However, it is possible to let service members reflect on these types of situations before they are confronted with them. This is what we intend to do with ethics education aimed at fostering moral competence. This type of education supports service members by supplying them with a new vocabulary that enables them to identify, discuss and learn from moral dilemmas from the past and to deal with present ones. Doing so will enable them, together with others, to relate to such dilemmas and decide on courses of action that are well-considered.

Literature

Annas, G.J. (2008). 'Military Medical Ethics – Physician First, Last, Always.' *New England Journal of Medicine, 359*(11), 1087–1090.

Aristotle, E.N. (1999). *Ethica Nicomachea*. Translated, introduced and annotated by Christine Pannier and Jean Verhaeghe. Groningen: Historische Uitgeverij.

Baarda, Th.A. van & Verweij, D.E.M. (eds.) (2006). *Military Ethics: The Dutch Approach. A Practical Guide*. Leiden: Martinus Nijhoff Publishers.

Baarle, E. van, Bosch, J., Widdershoven, G., Verweij, D. & Molewijk, B. (2015). 'Moral Dilemmas in a Military Context. A Case Study of a Train the Trainer Course on Military Ethics.' *Journal of Moral Education, 44*(4), 457–478.

Baarle, E. van, Hartman, L., Verweij, D., Molewijk, B. & Widdershoven, G. (2017). 'What Sticks? The Evaluation of a Train-the-Trainer Course in Military Ethics and Its Perceived Outcomes.' *Journal of Military Ethics, 16*(1–2), 56–77.

Baarle, E. van (2018). *Ethics Education in the Military: Fostering Reflective Practice and Moral Competence*, dissertation. Consulted on: https://research.vu.nl/en/publicati ons/ethics-education-in-the-military-fostering-reflective-practice-an.

Bentham, J. (1789). *An Introduction to the Principles of Morals*. London: Athlone.

Braak, I. van de (2011). *Inspireren tot medeverantwoordelijkheid. TGI als methodiek voor effectief leiderschap*. Amsterdam: Boom/Nelissen.

Cohn, R. (1976). *Von der Psychoanalyse zur themenzentrierten Interaktion*. Stuttgart: Ernst Klett Verlag.

Karssing, E. (2000). *Morele competenties in organisaties*. Assen: Van Gorcum.

Kant, I. (1785). *Fundamental Principles of the Metaphysic of Morals*. Raleigh, NC: Generic NL Freebook Publisher.

Kessels, J., Boers, E. & Mostert, P. (2002). *Vrije ruimte. Filosoferen in organisaties*. Amsterdam: Boom.

NRT (2017). *Kijken in de ziel: Op missie*. https://www.npostart.nl/kijken-in-de-ziel-mil itairen/07-08-2017/VPWON_1272714.

Olsthoorn, P. (2010). *Military Ethics and Virtues: An Interdisciplinary Approach for the 21st Century*. London: Routledge.

Robson, J.M. (1996). *Collected Works of John Stuart Mill (Vol. 8)*. London: Routledge.

Sherblom, S.A. (2012). 'What Develops in Moral Development? A Model of Moral Sensibility.' *Journal of Moral Education, 41*(1), 117–142.

Verweij, D. (2005). 'Het belang van militaire ethiek voor de krijgsmacht.' *Carré*, 7(8), 28–30.

Wortel, E., & Verweij, D. (2008). 'Inquiry, Criticism and Reasonableness: Socratic Dialogue as a Research Method?' *Practical Philosophy*, 9(2), 54–72.

Wortel, E., & Bosch, J. (2011). 'Strengthening Moral Competence: A 'Train the Trainer' Course on Military Ethics.' *Journal of Military Ethics*, 10(1), 17–35.

CHAPTER 3

'The Roof, the Roof, the Roof is on Fire'

Moral Standards and Moral Disengagement in Military Organisations

Eva van Baarle and Marjon Blom-Terhell

1 Introduction

In daily life, people do not always keep to moral standards and values, including the moral standards and values that they themselves consider important. This phenomenon is called the 'blurring of moral standards' and can be described as a process in which the behaviour of a certain group of people gradually, and sometimes unnoticed by those people themselves, becomes unacceptable (Vogelaar and Verweij 2009; Van Baarda 2006). To put it simply: moral standards gradually become invisible; i.e. they blur. As set out in Chapter 1, a moral standard can be seen as a rule, a certain guideline for action. Underlying those moral standards are values, ideals we pursue and that we find important and valuable. This means that if moral standards become blurred, values are also at stake. A blurring of moral standards therefore also implies a blurring of values. Instead of the 'blurring of moral standards or values', the phenomenon may also be referred to as 'moral disengagement' (Bandura 1999).

Past examples of moral standards becoming blurred can also be found at the Netherlands Defence organisation, both during deployments and in peacetime. Reports of incidents, hazing rituals, threats, mistreatment and indecent assaults at the Oranje Barracks in Schaarsbergen (Vermeer 2018) demonstrate that moral disengagement constitutes a real risk. Various cases of abuse and reports on the subject have raised awareness of the undesirable effects of a socially unsafe environment. The Dutch Safety Board's investigation into the fatal mortar accident in Mali in 2016 stresses that military culture makes asking critical questions more difficult (Dutch Safety Board 2017), which only increases the risk of a blurring of standards.

Military history provides several examples of moral disengagement, such as the violence by Dutch troops during the decolonisation war in Indonesia (1945–1949) (Limpach 2016, see also Chapter 4) and by Americans during their war against the communist insurgents in Vietnam (1965–1973), such as the massacre at My Lai (Bandura 2002, see also Chapter 4). The pictures of tortured Iraqi prisoners in Abu Ghraib prison in Iraq may also be mentioned in

© KONINKLIJKE BRILL NV, LEIDEN, 2022 | DOI:10.1163/9789004512474_004

this context (Zimbardo 2007). And more recently, the Brereton Reports conclusions regarding 'Questions of Unlawful Conduct concerning the Special Operations Task Group in Afghanistan' on the unlawfull killing of 39 people by 25 Australian Special Forces personnel, predominantly from the Special Air Service Regiment' (Brereton Report 2020).

These examples are extreme, but a blurring of standards often begins in small ways, in situations where it is not clear to everyone that standards are becoming blurred. For one person, certain behaviour is logical and appropriate to the situation, while for another the same behaviour is unacceptable because important values are at stake. Consider, for example, a drink-fuelled party that is threatening to get out of hand, where colleagues start shouting things that may be offensive. At what point do you speak up? At what point do values become violated? And which values are we talking about here? You may think to yourself: what's the big deal, it's all in good fun and boys will be boys? Or is this actually a situation where standards may become blurred?

In ethics education at the Defence organisation, students reflect on practical situations of this kind and assess whether a blurring of standards can be said to apply, and if so, why this is the case and what the options are for dealing with it (Wortel and Bosch 2011). In this way, we help raise awareness of the risks that can lead to moral disengagement. Students learn to recognise situations in which values are at stake. Dialogue is seen as a vehicle for joint moral learning and developing normative conclusions (Van Baarle 2018). In this chapter we work in a similar way. Based on a real-life case from military practice, we look at how a blurring of standards can be recognised. In this context, we will discuss eight factors that can be used for that purpose (Bandura 1999). We will then address the question of how to counteract any blurring of standards and how an organisation can learn from incidents. The concept of 'just culture' will be introduced to refer to a culture of fairness, where the promotion of cooperation is paramount and where co-workers feel safe to raise issues and discuss them. Dialogue and looking for improvement together also play an important role here. In addition, we discuss what a leader can do to promote a learning culture.

2 'Week Review' Case

Below, we present an example from military practice that has been extensively covered in Dutch newspaper NRC (Versteegh 2018a; Versteegh 2018b). It should be noted that the videos and music fragments referred to in the case are also frequently mentioned by students in ethics education classes in the Defence organisation. A striking aspect is that students indicate that the case is a difficult subject to bring up for discussion and that in practice they have often failed to do so themselves.

Based on the publication in NRC (Versteegh 2018a; Versteegh 2018b) we made a 'thick' description (Ponterotto 2006) of the case. A thick description of an event makes it possible to experience the complexity of an issue. We will then discuss the case with the help of the aforementioned eight factors that can be used to recognise moral disengagement (Bandura 1999).

During your deployment to Jordan, at the weekly informal gathering known as the Week Review in one of the army tents on the compound, you get to see images of bombardments accompanied by rousing music. The images are spectacular. They may be the bombs that you mounted under an F16. Is that a body you see? The images fill you with a sense of pride: we're successfully pushing back the caliphate. There's cheering in the tent. Should you join in?

The idea behind the Week Review is that the entire detachment is kept abreast of progress in the aerial war. The images were taken with cameras mounted under the F16s. The purpose of the video footage is to see whether the targets have been hit and whether there have been civilian casualties. Watching these images together creates an intense feeling of group solidarity; we're doing this together and we're successful. You don't want to detract from that feeling. However, it seems as if more and more creativity is being put into spicing up the footage with rock songs with 'fitting' lyrics. 'The roof, the roof, the roof is on fire, we don't need no water let the motherfucker burn, burn motherfucker, burn!' booms from the speakers – the chorus from the song 'Fire Water Burn' from rock band Bloodhound Gang. Everybody is singing along. What song will they add next week? Around you, colleagues are watching the images with a look of amusement. Is this acceptable? If so, why? Or maybe it's not? It does feel somewhat uncomfortable, but then, who am I to make a fuss about it? Just imagine the reaction from those pilots if I say something about it. And I really don't fancy being a moral crusader anyway. Besides, everyone else seems to be fine with it. I don't even know myself why I'm feeling uncomfortable. After all, doesn't the system ensure that we don't take out anything that's not a military target? Aren't civilian casualties simply 'collateral damage' then? Or maybe this fits in just too well with the aggressive military slang I've been hearing more and more the last few weeks, like 'blowing Ahmed out of his flip-flops'? On the other hand, we're acting against people who do the most horrible things. Just think of the Jordanian pilot who was captured by IS and burned alive in an iron cage while the camera was running. Images still etched in your mind. Our pilots should be allowed to let off steam a little, and they can afford a bit more than the rest; after all, they're the ones taking the real risks.

3   Recognising Moral Disengagement: Eight Factors

The Canadian psychologist Albert Bandura describes eight factors used to justify behaviour (Bandura 1999). It should be noted that if one or more of these factors exists, that does not necessarily mean that there is a blurring of standards. Although Bandura argues that these factors are excuses that are used, we would not wish to prematurely rule out the possibility that they may constitute legitimate arguments. In addition, a number of these factors could also be seen as coping strategies, i.e. strategies and (stress) responses used by people to cope with difficult situations and to keep functioning normally (Lazarus 1993; Nilsson et al. 2011). There is also a 'dark' side to these mechanisms, which can lead to a blurring of standards (De Graaff et al. 2016). These eight factors can be used as alarm bells to investigate what is going on in a situation, to assess whether there are risks of standards becoming blurred and to determine how to deal with these responsibly.

The eight factors are further explained below, on the basis of the case above as well as with the help of other examples from military practice. We then discuss whether the case involves moral disengagement.

Moral justification means that those involved in particular behaviour justify it to themselves. A person usually knows on the basis of his/her own values and moral standards whether an action is wrong or incorrect. Moral justification means that a person changes this original belief and thereby condones the action. Moral justification often occurs when a higher goal is pursued and the means to achieve that goal are no longer critically considered. For example, an athlete who justifies using doping for the achievement of a higher goal: performing better in his sport and winning a race. The end thus justifies the means. Moral justification is also involved in the use of force. Force is used on the assumption that there is no alternative and then becomes purely instrumental. In the case given above, it is put like this: 'Watching these images together creates an intense feeling of group solidarity; we're doing this together *and* we're successful. You don't want to detract from that feeling.' Promoting comradeship and group solidarity is important. The question is whether showing these images in combination with rousing music and lyrics is the necessary means to achieve this end. The argumentation in the last part of the thick description also tends towards moral justification, in any event of the pilots' conduct: 'Our pilots should be allowed to let off steam a little, and they can afford a bit more than the rest; after all, they're the ones taking the real risks.'

3.1 Euphemistic Language

Using veiled language is also referred to as euphemistic labelling. Such language may serve to mislead outsiders, but may also be used by speakers to reassure themselves. Words are used that conceal the seriousness of the situation. In the case described, the term 'collateral damage' could be seen as a euphemism that masks the human tragedy of innocent victims. In the context of moral disengagement, it is interesting to find out to what extent the use of language can still be considered 'normal', acceptable or functional and to what extent certain terms contribute to a process of moral disengagement.

3.2 Advantageous Comparison

An advantageous or favourable comparison means that a situation or one's own behaviour is compared to a situation or behaviour that is much worse, so that one's own action compares favourably with it. Colleagues who go home earlier on Fridays than the agreed time can justify this by, for example, pointing out that certain other colleagues went home much earlier. In that case, leaving an hour earlier is not so bad, is it? This mechanism can also play a role during hazing rituals. If colleagues have undergone a tough hazing themselves, this may become an excuse to subject novices to severe treatment, too.

In the case described, the advantageous comparison is also used. A comparison is made with IS: 'Just think of the Jordanian pilot who was captured by IS and burned alive in an iron cage while the camera was running', which makes putting music to videos during the 'Week Review' look rather innocent.

3.3 Displacement of Responsibility

Shifting or passing on of responsibility ('displacement') occurs in various ways. Firstly, by shifting responsibility to an authority or someone in a senior position. Secondly, by pointing to the group or fellow group members and, finally, by referring to the situation.

The research into obedience to authority conducted by psychologist Stanley Milgram (Milgram 1974) shows that people are more willing to carry out actions if they are instructed to do so by a leader or other authority figure. In that case, people feel less responsible for their actions. The research shows that people will obey (what they perceive as) a legitimate authority, even if the action in question goes against their own conscience. In a number of experiments Milgram had a subject ask questions to a second subject (in reality an actor), who was in another room. For every incorrect answer, electrical shocks of incrementally increasing voltage had to be administered (up to a maximum voltage of 450 v). Unbeknownst to the first subjects, however, no electrical shocks were actually administered, with the actors only pretending to be in pain. The research was supposedly about learning under pressure (this was told to the first subject), but in reality the research was about the influence of authority, and whether a researcher's authority could induce a person to cross his/her moral boundaries. The outcome was shocking: about 65 percent of the subjects kept on 'administering shocks' until a lethal level was reached (Milgram 1974).

In hierarchical organisations such as the Defence organisation, the displacement of responsibility can create a significant risk of moral disengagement. This likely also played a role in the case described. If it was a pilot who started the video, that alone could have made it difficult for (lower-ranking) support personnel to broach the subject.

It is tempting to pass on responsibility to fellow group members. 'If everyone's doing it, you just go along with it.' 'Everyone else seems to be fine with it.' When an entire group is cheering along, it is difficult to be the only one voicing a dissenting opinion. The experiments conducted by psychologist Solomon Asch into conformism and peer pressure show the great extent to which people are willing to conform to the group's views. He shows that even if people are able to see that the group's opinion with regard to the length of a number of lines is evidently incorrect, they are still inclined to conform to the group's views on the subject (Asch 1951; Levine 1999).

In addition to passing on responsibility to a higher authority or to peers, it is also possible to shift responsibility to a state of consciousness or to a situation that got out of hand. In the case at hand the responsibility is also shifted in part by invoking stress and the need to let off steam together from time to time.

3.4   *Diffusion of Responsibility*

Diffusion of responsibility arises, for example, when the work is divided; each individual task is relatively innocent, but this is not the case when looking at the greater whole. One could think, for example, of the use of WhatsApp groups: pictures or videos that are intended to be funny are posted and thumbs-up signs, emojis and sometimes texts are added by recipients. If increasingly coarse jokes are being made in WhatsApp groups, at some point even culminating in the sharing of racist and pornographic images with references to Nazi Germany (*De Telegraaf* 2018), who can be held responsible? The person who posts the content? Or those who view it and forward it? It may also be the case that no one at all feels responsible anymore and that the risk of moral disengagement increases further as a result.

Regarding the 'Week Review' we can also ask ourselves: who is responsible for this Week Review? Is that clear in this situation? Is it the pilots? The detachment, or everyone present? Or is it mainly the commander?

3.5 *Disregarding and Denial of Injurious Effects*

Disregarding or downplaying effects can make it easier not to act, or to undertake a harmful action yourself. Cultural relativism could also be regarded as the downplaying of effects. An example of such relativism regards the phenomenon of *'chai boys'*: some of the Dutch personnel deployed to Afghanistan came home with stories about dancing boys, flower boys, catamites or *'chai boys'* (tea boys). Boys wearing make-up engaged as help to, for example, police and army commanders, and who do more 'chores' than pouring tea. They also have to perform sexual services. Sometimes they are 'lent' to other powerful men for sexual services. The boys, sometimes not older than eleven, are chosen for their height and good looks. The more attractive the boy, the more prestige one acquires. The practice is officially forbidden in Afghanistan, but unfortunately the legislation in question does not prevent abuse of boys from occurring (just as in other countries). A number of Dutch personnel who were confronted with this practice in Afghanistan argued that this phenomenon was simply part of the culture (Schut and Van Baarle 2017). In doing so, they implied that different cultures have different moral standards and values and that it would be an imperialistic notion to say that people in Afghanistan should adapt to our (Western) moral standards and values.

The use of cultural relativistic arguments of this sort could also be seen as a way of dealing with one's own powerlessness and as a coping strategy (Whetham 2008; De Graaff et al. 2016; Schut and Van Baarle 2017). During the work-up programme for Afghanistan, it was explicitly stated that it was forbidden to question this phenomenon because of possible political repercussions. It is easy to imagine the powerlessness that this creates; as an individual service member it is practically impossible to exert influence (see also Chapter 5 on the potentially drastic moral-psychological effects of these types of phenomena).

The 'Week Review' case is different, because this is organised by colleagues. In that case it is quite possible that several other colleagues feel uncomfortable. By not raising the issue, they downplay or ignore their moral intuition and push their feeling of discomfort aside. There could also be a question of disregarding or downplaying the injurious effects: those present may suffer damage, because, as a result of peer pressure, they respond differently to the images than they would normally. In doing so, they unconsciously exceed their own personal boundaries.

3.6 *Dehumanisation*

Dehumanisation means that you no longer see others as real human beings. One form of dehumanisation is the use of derogatory language as the norm to designate certain people, such as slant-eye, cockroach, rat or towel head. Comments from the case such as 'we're going to blow Ahmed out of his flip-flops' fall into this category. This could also be seen as a coping function to enable one to kill an opponent (Bandura 1999). Sometimes words are simply jargon. The Defence organisation uses a great deal of jargon, with its own unique terms and many abbreviations. Examples are the word 'mutant' for an injured person and PAX (Personnel Assigned to Exercise) for personnel. This raises the question of when language can still be called functional and when a real risk of moral disengagement can be said to exist.

3.7 *Blaming the Victim*

By arguing that the victim of a crime has himself to blame, a perpetrator can justify his own behaviour. Examples of cases in which the blame is sometimes placed on the victim are indecent assault or rape cases. A victim's behaviour or style of dress is then labelled as provocative and presented as an excuse: she should have known better than to wear such a short skirt. This factor is represented less obviously in the case. It could be argued that causing civilian casualties can be justified using this factor, thus seemingly condoning it and increasing the risk of collateral damage as a result. They were 'in the wrong place at the wrong time'.

Bandura argues that these eight factors enable people to distance themselves from their own behaviour in order to be able to accept certain actions and behaviour. This is a very gradual, and often unconscious, process. The repeated toleration of this behaviour and failure to raise it for discussion, both by the leader and by personnel (e.g. because of loyalty), can lead to a downward spiral of moral disengagement. There may also be callousness or numbness as a result of the idea that something has to be thought of as 'normal'.

4 Moral Disengagement and Organisational Learning

When considering instances in which different aspects of moral disengagement are involved, many students feel the need for a judgment: is this really a case of moral disengagement? They need an objective opinion of what happened. The question of accountability or imputation also seems to play a role. In practice, it is very difficult to establish *the* objective boundary or opinion regarding these types of situations, and perhaps such a boundary does not exist. A characteristic of moral issues is that it is not always possible to make a clear-cut distinction between right and wrong. It seems more important to engage in discussion with each other, from different perspectives, on where the boundaries lie and why that is the case. The real art is to let students iden-tify exactly what is at stake in a given case and to talk about it and investigate it together. What is the concern? Is there room to discuss it?

The above analysis of the case shows that a number of the factors, or alarm bells, that Bandura describes play a role in the 'Week Review' case. However, the notion that risks of moral disengagement play a role in this case does not necessarily mean that there actually *is* moral disengagement. Exactly what moral standards and values are at stake? Why do a number of colleagues feel uncomfortable in this situation? Where does the need come from to watch this type of footage together and put music to the videos?

Music can play an important role in boosting morale, strengthening bonds between personnel and letting off steam over the stress of fighting a brutal opponent. As Niels Roelen put it in NRC:

> We are a war force in the garb of peace, forbidden from saying out loud what we are doing. We send people to areas where ethics sometimes become subordinate to the survival instinct and where you neutralise opponents by killing them. The assignments carried out during a mission leave no service member untouched; soldiers are people and not robots.
>
> For me to stay human in Afghanistan, I needed music – including provocative music. That music helped me deal with aggression, pain, sadness and stress. It helped me to protect myself, distance myself from the killing of another human being – particularly by adding effects like in a movie.
>
> ROELEN 2018

Yet there are also colleagues who feel uncomfortable with this kind of music during the Week Review, without being able to explain to themselves exactly why. Notably, the feeling of discomfort does not only arise from the Week Review, but goes hand in hand with multiple other signals. In the case, the soldier's jargon 'blowing Ahmed out of his flip-flops' is also mentioned.

You could say soldiers need to be able to strike a balancing act. In order for soldiers to be able to kill, a certain form of dehumanisation is functional, but at the same time they must also be capable of 'humanising'. Soldiers must abide by law of war. In addition, 'humanisation' is important when working with local counterparts and in winning of hearts and minds of the local popula-tion (French and Jack 2015). How do you organise that balancing act with each other? Or: how do you teach each other to strike a balancing act? The 'Week Review' example is interesting because personnel organise it themselves and have a say in it. The example of the chai boys described above is a lot more complicated in that respect.

When the 'Week Review' was reported in the media, an inclination towards decisive action was evident: for example, by making new rules. In the same article in NRC it emerged that the Defence organisation no longer wanted any music to be added to videos showing arms deployment (Versteegh 2018b). You may wonder whether this was because of the moral disengagement or because of the impact of the NRC article and the political pressure that arose in its wake. Creating more rules in an organisation may provide some guidance, but, as noted in Chapter 1, it is impossible to capture everything in rules (cf. also Paine 1994). It is also important to have a mindset *and* a culture in which it is normal to bring up issues for discussion in spite of the hierarchy. To take the case example, someone from 'maintenance' should also be able to talk about the issue with a pilot. There will always be a certain tension in hierarchical organisations with regard to discussing (sensitive) issues with those of higher rank. That does not mean, however, that we should not strive to enable sensitive issues to be discussed. Where moral-ethical issues are concerned, we can all learn from each other.

An interesting question to answer would be why Defence personnel turned to NRC following their 'Week Review' experience. Below we discuss this question from a 'just culture' perspective on organisational learning, in which dialogue and looking for improvement together take a central role. We also discuss the role of the leader in promoting a learning culture.

4.1 A 'Just Culture' Perspective

What can an organisation learn from situations such as the 'Week Review'? In relation to organisational learning, Sidney Dekker introduces the concept of a restorative 'just culture' (Dekker 2009; 2012; Dekker and Breakey 2016). This restorative approach requires a non-retributive approach to situations such as the 'Week Review'. A retributive approach would entail the questions that are usually asked first of all: 'Who did this? What rule was broken? How serious is the offence and what would be an appropriate retribution?' In an approach where restoration and learning are central, one is mainly concerned with questions such as: who has been harmed? What do they need? Who is responsible for providing them with that? What role do the organisation and the environment play in learning from this situation? Looking at the case from that perspective, the questions could be: what does the detachment need? What need is met by adding music to the images? Does music serve to express a certain feeling? Is that something that could be discussed?

In a retributive view of learning, human error is seen as the cause of incidents. To remedy the incident we focus on the individual who caused it: remove the rotten apple and the problem is solved. From a 'just culture' perspective, human error is not a cause but rather a symptom. In finding a solution, we should look at the system (including procedures and cultural elements). An individual is always part of a certain system. The system creates contextual conditions that cause an individual to think that his or her behaviour is logical or appropriate to the situation. If this leads to an incident, the first question should be: what can we learn from this for the future? What changes can we make to reduce the likelihood of the problem recurring? Dialogue should be conducted in such a way that participants do not feel threatened but appreciated, even if things have gone wrong.

Promoting a 'just culture' is intended to create an environment where personnel feel safe enough to raise issues and discuss them. Dialogue and looking for improvement together are of central importance here. An important element of a 'just culture' is a feeling among employees that they can contribute to a dialogue or ask a critical question without this having negative consequences. Such negative consequences could affect their self-image, social status or career (Kahn 1990; Edmondson 1999). Amy Edmondson has termed this 'psychological safety': a reciprocal feeling in which the participants perceive a group or team as safe enough for them to take risks, for example by speaking up (Edmondson 1999; 2004). To what extent do these colleagues feel safe enough to try and speak about their discomfort? Social safety is a broad concept that is connected to factors such as human resource policies, organisational structure and culture; psychological safety is also part of it.

In recent years a great deal of research has been conducted into the willingness on the part of employees to report unsafe situations. Examples include 'speaking up' as part of a safety culture (Edmondson 2003; Okuyama et al. 2014; Schwappach and Richard 2018). A great deal of attention is already being devoted to this in the air force (Catino & Patriotta 2013). For example, use is made of the team concept of Crew Resource Management (CRM). The goal of CRM is to ensure the best possible information exchange, which forms the basis of obtaining a shared picture of a situation and decision making with broad support. Part of the speaking-up culture in the air force is the standard debriefing after each flight, in which all crew members have a role. The morning after a debriefing a second learning moment is held, i.e. a morning briefing, and in the event of night sorties there is an extra afternoon briefing, too. In addition to the weather and open airfields, experiences are also discussed.

The importance of speaking up also applies to situations that at first sight appear to bear a less direct relationship to physical safety, or that less obviously involve an 'error'. Speaking up can be relevant in recognising risks of moral disengagement in time and in helping each other to stay alert to those risks, as well as in preventing incidents. Past experiences with speaking up in the organisation may support this. Research into psychological safety shows that leader behaviour has a great deal of influence on the willingness, or lack of willingness, of employees to raise something for discussion (Alingh et al. 2019). A leader can lower the threshold for employees for speaking up in a number of ways: first of all by signalling the complexity inherent in the work of the Defence organisation and the risks of moral disengagement to which this may give rise. Secondly, by pointing out that a leader is also a human being, and therefore fallible. Critical questions and signals from personnel are necessary in order for everyone to stay alert to the risk of moral disengagement. Leaders should invite personnel explicitly to ask such questions and give such signals. However, it is not only the invitation that matters but also giving an explicitly appreciative rather than defensive response to critical questions or signals (Edmondson 2018). That would appear to be self-evident, but it certainly is not. This attitude of leaders is also referred to as moral leadership. It is about the ability to have discussions with others and thus form an opinion about moral issues, about where boundaries lie, in order to jointly decide whether or not to change practices (Solinger et al. 2019). Moral leadership does not evolve from a top-down process; rather, it is something relational and requires moral courage. It is about interactions between people, for example reflecting with each other on situations such as the 'Week Review'.

5 Conclusion

Moral disengagement – the process by which the behaviour of a certain group of people gradually, and sometimes without being noticed, becomes unacceptable – poses a risk at the Defence organisation, as it does in other organisations. Moral disengagement often starts in small ways, in situations where it is not immediately clear to all that moral standards and values are at risk of being violated. It is precisely this type of situation that is discussed during ethics education at the Defence organisation. This chapter focused on a real case from military practice: the 'Week Review'. Based on this example, we discussed eight factors that can be used to recognise moral disengagement. We then addressed the question of how achieving a 'just culture' could contribute to recognising and counteracting moral disengagement. In a 'just culture' perspective, dialogue and looking for improvement together are of central importance. Particularly in the air force, a great deal of experience has already been gathered with 'crew resource management' and 'speaking up', both of which concepts tie in with a 'just culture' perspective on organisational learning. Such experience is also important in situations that at first sight appear to bear a less direct relationship to physical safety, or that less obviously involve an 'error'. In such situations, the importance lies in recognising risks of moral disengagement in time.

Acknowledgements

We would like to thank the following people for their valuable feedback on an earlier version of this chapter: Marsha Meijer, working at the Central Defence Integrity Organisation; Lieutenant Colonel Leonie Boskeljon, Senior Pilot Psychologist and Human Factor Specialist; and Colonel Michel de Rivecourt, Head of the Safety Staff Group within Air Force Command.

Literature

Alingh, C., Wijngaarden, J. van, Voorde, K. van de, Paauwe, J. and Huijsman, R. (2019). 'Speaking Up about Patient Safety Concerns: The Influence of Safety Management Approaches and Climate on Nurses' Willingness to Speak Up.' *BMJ Quality & Safety*, 28(1):39–48. DOI: 10.1136/bmjqs-2017-007163.

Asch, S.E. (1951). 'Effects of Group Pressure Upon the Modification and Distortion of Judgments.' In: H. Guetzkow (ed.), *Groups, Leadership, and Men* (p. 177–190). Pittsburgh, PA: Carnegie.

Baarda, Th.A. van & Verweij, D.E.M. (eds.) (2006). Military Ethics: The Dutch Approach. A Practical Guide. Leiden: Martinus Nijhoff Publishers.

Baarle, E.M. van (2018). *Ethics Education in the Military: Fostering Reflective Practice and Moral Competence*, dissertation. Consulted on: https://research.vu.nl/en/publications/ethics-education-in-the-military-fostering-reflective-practice-an.

Bandura, A. (1990). 'Selective Activation and Disengagement of Moral Control.' *Journal of Social Issues. vol. 46 no. 1*, 27–46.

Bandura, A. (1999) 'Moral Disengagement in the Perpetration of Inhumanities.' *Personality and Social Psychology Review, vol. 3 no. 3*, 193–209.

Bandura, A. (2002). 'Selective Moral Disengagement in the Exercise of Moral Agency.' *Journal of Moral Education, 31(2)*, 101–119.

Brereton Report. (2020) Inspector-General of the Australian Defence Force Afghanistan Inquiry Report. Consulted on: https://afghanistaninquiry.defence.gov.au/sites/default/files/2020-11/IGADF-Afghanistan-Inquiry-Public-Release-Version.pdf.

Catino, M., Patriotta, G. (2013). 'Learning from Errors: Cognition, Emotions and Safety Culture in the Italian Air Force.' *Organization Studies, 34*(4), 437–467.

'Defensie onderzoekt nazi-uitingen.' *De Telegraaf,* 13-9-2018): https://www.telegraaf.nl/nieuws/2914769/defensie-onderzoekt- nazi-uitingen.

Dekker, S. (2009). 'Just Culture: Who Gets to Draw the Line?' *Cognition, Technology & Work 11*:177–185. DOI: 10.1007/s10111-008-0110-7.

Dekker, S. (2012). *Just Culture: Balancing Safety and Accountability.* Boca Raton, FL: CRC Press.

Dekker, Sidney W.A. and Breakey, H. (2016). '"Just Culture:' Improving Safety by Achieving Substantive, Procedural and Restorative Justice.' *Safety Science 85*:187–193. DOI: https://doi.org/10.1016/j.ssci.2016.01.018.

Dutch Safety Board. (2017). Mortar Accident Mali. The Hague: Dutch Safety Board. Consulted on: file:///C:/Users/Admin/AppData/Local/Temp/d863a531ee8ddef _20172954_engelse_samenvatting_rapportage_mali_171214.pdf.

Edmondson, A.C. (1999). 'Psychological Safety and Learning Behavior in Work Teams.' *Administrative Science Quarterly, 44*(2), 350–383.

Edmondson, A.C. (2003). 'Speaking Up in the Operating Room: How Team Leaders Promote Learning in Interdisciplinary Action Teams.' *Journal of management studies, 40*(6), 1419–1452.

Edmondson, Amy C. (2004). 'Psychological Safety, Trust, and Learning in Organizations: A Group-level Lens.' In: R.M. Kramer and K.S. Cook (eds.), *Trust and Distrust in Organizations: Dilemmas and Approaches.* New York: Russell Sage Foundation.

Edmondson, A.C. (2018). *The Fearless Organization: Creating Psychological Safety in the Workplace for Learning, Innovation, and Growth.* Hoboken, NJ: John Wiley & Sons.

French, S.E. and Jack, A.I. (2015). 'Dehumanizing the Enemy: The Intersection of Neuroethics and Military Ethics.' In: *The Responsibility to Protect: Alternative Perspectives. International Studies on Military Ethics, Volume: 1.* Leiden: Brill Nijhoff.

Graaff, M.C. de, Schut, M., Verweij, D.E., Vermetten, E. and Giebels, E. (2016). 'Emotional Reactions and Moral Judgment: The Effects of Morally Challenging Interactions in Military Operations.' *Ethics & behavior, 26*(1), 14–31.

Kahn, W.A. (1990). 'Psychological Conditions of Personal Engagement and Disengagement at Work.' *Academy of Management Journal, 33*(4), 692–724.

Lazarus, R.S. (1993). *Coping Theory and Research: Past, Present, and Future. Fifty Years of the Research and Theory of RS Lazarus: An Analysis of Historical and Perennial Issues,* 366–388.

Levine, J.M. (1999). 'Solomon Asch's Legacy for Group Research.' *Personality and Social Psychology Review, 3*(4), 358–364.

Limpach, R. (2016). *De brandende kampongs van Generaal Spoor.* Amsterdam: Boom.

Milgram, S. (1974). *Obedience to Authority: An Experimental View*. New York: Harper & Row.

Nilsson, S., Sjöberg, M., Kallenberg, K. and Larsson, G. (2011). 'Moral Stress in International Humanitarian Aid and Rescue Operations: A Grounded Theory Study.' *Ethics & Behavior*, 21(1), 49–68.

Okuyama, A., Wagner, C. and Bijnen, B. (2014). 'Speaking Up for Patient Safety by Hospital-based Health Care Professionals: A Literature Review'. *BMC Health Services Research*, 14(1), 61. https://doi.org/10.1186/1472-6963-14-61.

Onderzoeksraad voor Veiligheid, 'Mortierongeval Mali' (September 2017): https://www.onderzoeksraad.nl/uploads/phase-docs/1662/187c7ff6dc04hoofdrapport-mortierongeval-mali-nl.pdf.

Paine, L.S. (1994). 'Managing for Organizational Integrity.' *Harvard Business Review*, 72(2), 106–117.

Ponterotto, J.G. (2006). 'Brief Note on the Origins, Evolution, and Meaning of the Qualitative Research Concept 'Thick Description'.' *The Qualitative Report*, 11: 538–549.

Roelen, Niels (2018). 'Muziek hielp mij als officier omgaan met agressie en verdriet.' *NRC*, 15-10-2018: https://www.nrc.nl/nieuws/2018/10/15/in-uruzgan-had-ik-muziek-nodig-ook-onfatsoenlijke-a2556085.

Schut, M. and Baarle, E. van (2017). 'Dancing Boys and the Moral Dilemmas of Military Missions: The Practice of Bacha Bazi in Afghanistan.' In: Bah, Abu B. (ed.), *International Security and Peacebuilding: Africa, the Middle East, and Europe*, 77–98. Bloomington: Indiana University Press.

Schwappach, D. and Richard, A. (2018). Speak Up-related Climate and Its Association with Healthcare Workers' Speaking Up and Withholding Voice Behaviours: A Cross-sectional Survey in Switzerland. *BMJ Qual Saf*, 27(10), 827–835.

Solinger, O.N., Jansen, P.G. and Cornelissen, J. (2019). 'The Emergence of Moral Leadership.' *Academy of Management Review*, DOI: https://doi.org/10.5465/amr.2016.0263.

Vermeer, O. (2018). 'Vijf militairen vervolgd voor misstanden op kazerne.' *NRC*, 9-12-2018: https://www.nrc.nl/nieuws/2018/09/12/schaarsbergen-vijf-militairen-vervolgd-voor-misstanden-op-kazerne-a1616191.

Versteegh, K. (2018a). 'Slaapgebrek, macho-rock en bommen gooien.' *NRC*, 9-7-2018: https://www.nrc.nl/nieuws/2018/09/07/slaap-gebrek-macho-rock-en-bommen-de-nederlandse-strijd-tegen-is-a1615751.

Versteegh, K. (2018b). 'Defensie verbiedt rock onder filmpjes.' *NRC*, 10-8-2018: https://www.nrc.nl/nieuws/2018/10/08/defensie- verbiedt-rock-onder-filmpjes-a2417193.

Vogelaar, A.L.W. and Verweij, D.E.M. (2009). 'Normvervaging.' In: R. Moelker, J. Noll and M. de Weger (eds.), *Krijgsmacht en samenleving. Over de inzet van een geweldsinstrument: bestuurlijke, politieke en veiligheidsaspecten*. Amsterdam: Boom.

Whetham, D. (2008). 'The Challenge of Ethical Relativism in a Coalition Environment.' *Journal of Military Ethics*, 7, 302–316.

Wortel, E., & Bosch, J. (2011). Strengthening moral competence: a 'train the trainer'course on military ethics. *Journal of Military Ethics*, 10(1), 17–35.

Zimbardo, P.G. (2007). *The Lucifer effect: understanding how good people turn evil.* New York: Random House.

CHAPTER 4

Loyalty

A Grey Virtue?

Peter Olsthoorn and Marjon Blom-Terhell

1 Introduction

In the early morning of 16 March 1968 a US Army company left for the village of My Lai (better known among the Americans as Pinkville). The village was supposedly full of Viet Cong fighters and sympathisers, but on arrival that turned out not to be the case. Despite the absence of any armed resistance, the American soldiers, led by Lieutenant William Calley, began to execute the defenceless population in groups. In the end, about four hundred civilians were killed. Strikingly, no less than two-thirds of the company's troops participated in the killing (McDermott and Hart, 2017, p.27). Helicopter pilot Hugh Thompson Jr. flew over the village that day and saw, in addition to the dozens of dead, how the surviving villagers were herded together and killed. Thompson landed his helicopter between some of his American colleagues and a group of fleeing Vietnamese, because it was clear that the latter group was about to be killed by the first. Before he disembarked, Thompson ordered his crew members to fire on their own troops if they did not stop shooting the villagers. Thompson eventually succeeded in rescuing this group. The fact that it was a relative outsider like Thompson who intervened should come as no surprise: in many cases of moral disengagement (see Chapter 3), someone external, who is therefore not part of the group, is the first to see that something is wrong.

Thompson reported on the massacre that same day. The US military initially tried to cover up this story for quite some time, and was more or less successful, until other US service personnel also informed journalists and politicians about the events. Thompson is now seen as a hero, and has been decorated for his role. That story is quite well-known now. Less known, however, is the fact that he had to wait thirty years for it. His intervention and reporting on colleagues was viewed initially with nothing but disapproval. Thompson was threatened for years afterwards and his career was sidelined. He was given the most dangerous assignments and was shot down four times in Vietnam. In the opinion of Mendel Rivers, Chairman of the House Armed Services Committee,

© KONINKLIJKE BRILL NV, LEIDEN, 2022 | DOI:10.1163/9789004512474_005

LOYALTY   41

the only person deserving of punishment for My Lai was Thompson (see, *inter alia*, Angers 2014). In the meantime, the real culprits remained virtually unpunished, partly due to pressure from public opinion. Thompson was rehabilitated only much later, and went on to give lectures to US Armed Forces audiences about the importance of moral courage. Only one of the perpetrators, Lieutenant Calley, was sentenced to prison. Again under pressure from public opinion, his prison sentence was soon commuted to house arrest by President Nixon.

Ten months after the My Lai massacre (but about ten months before that massacre finally made the news), on Friday 17 January 1969, Dutch psychologist and former conscript Joop Hueting gave a television interview. In this interview, the former conscript recounted how Dutch soldiers committed serious war crimes in the Netherlands East Indies in the years following the Second World War, such as shooting innocent civilians and mistreating detainees. Hueting: 'An example – we got POWs and they were shot several times, the catchword being: "Go and have a piss," whereupon they turned around and were shot in the back.' Another incident occurred when Hueting and his colleagues

> arrived at a *kampong*, in the middle of which was a little house. Two of our boys, a corporal and a private went inside, and the corporal emptied his submachine gun there. I went inside and in the half-light I saw fifteen, twenty people, women, children and men. When I was accustomed to the dark, I saw blood spurting from arterial wounds, screaming, mortal agony and the dying screams from the people in that house. And the guys outside were yelling at us: 'Can you be careful please, you're gonna shoot us in the butt right through that wall.'[1]

Hueting, who admits that his own actions in the former Dutch colony were not beyond reproach, emphasised that such cases were not incidents, but more common occurrences. Hueting's revelations about the misconduct of Dutch soldiers during the so-called 'police actions' came after more than twenty years of silence about the dubious goings-on at the time. Letters previously written to newspapers by Hueting were never published. What makes him special is that he did not give up and kept on telling the story that nobody wanted to hear.

---

1   These quotes from Hueting can be found here: https://anderetijden.nl/programma/1/And ere-Tijden/aflevering/551/De-excessennota.

Particularly striking were the often downright negative reactions to the interview. A few days afterwards, a major newspaper denounced the television appearance in a chief editorial comment. According to the morning paper, 'Mr Hueting's utterly senseless, disproportionate highlighting of incidental atrocities is reprehensible'. What had an even greater impact on Hueting was the fact that many veterans were furious, and even threatened him. Hueting was even forced to go into hiding with his family in a rural area, the Veluwe, and his children went to school under police escort.[2] Hueting died in late 2018, but appeared posthumously in a documentary series in which Hueting and other East Indies veterans talk about their experiences during those 'police actions'. Some of Hueting's former colleagues were now more open about the things that went wrong. Remarkably however, almost all veterans who talked in the series about Hueting's interview were still angry with him.[3]

What happened to Hueting brings us to an important point: in much of the literature dealing with matters such as integrity and moral courage, sticking to your beliefs is rewarded. The person who keeps to his or her principles will, albeit after suffering some discomfort, be held in esteem by the authorities, keep his or her job or even be promoted.[4] In the real world, however, things often turn out badly for people who stand up for their principles against the interests of the organisation and their colleagues. At best they are ignored, but sometimes they have to fear for their lives and go into hiding. Significantly, many whistleblowers strongly advise others not to take similar steps. A report on (the lack of) social safety at the Dutch Defence organisation also concludes that not reporting abuses is the sensible choice for Defence personnel. This is not a recommendation but rather a factual conclusion: 'More than 75% of people who reported to the committee indicated that whistleblowing – whether about socially undesirable behaviour or matters of professional integrity – resulted in (more) disadvantageous treatment' (Giebels, Van Oostrum and Van den Bos 2018, p. 17). Such disadvantageous treatment may consist, for example, of public humiliation whereby the loyalty and reliability of the whistleblower is questioned (Giebels, Van Oostrum and Van den Bos 2018, p.18). The report therefore found that there appears to be a good chance 'that whistleblowing or

---

2   Hueting's television appearances led to the so-called '*Excessennota*' (Excesses Memorandum), the Dutch government's first investigation into the decolonisation war in the Netherlands East Indies.

3   NPO, *Onze jongens op Java*, episode 3, available for viewing at https://www.npostart.nl/onze -jongens-op-java/05-12-2019/BV_101395136.

4   Rushworth Kidder's *Moral Courage* (2005) is full of such examples, where all ends well for everyone involved.

filing a complaint actually means the end of your career' within the Defence organisation (Giebels, Van Oostrum and Van den Bos 2018, p. 63). Until that situation changes, attempts to increase the willingness to report seem doomed to failure (and perhaps irresponsible, too). The fundamental question arising here is why someone who legitimately and for good reason calls attention to an abuse mainly suffers disadvantage as a result. Although that question cannot be answered unequivocally, loyalty often seems to play a major role in this respect. The whistleblower is not only blamed for the 'damage' done to the interest of the group or organisation, but also and particularly for being disloyal. Disloyalty appears to provoke universal disapproval: a disloyal Nazi might thus provoke more antipathy than a loyal one (Ewin 1992). But if disloyalty is so reprehensible, does that imply that loyalty is always good?

The remainder of this chapter addresses that virtue of loyalty – if the term 'virtue' is even appropriate here – and the role loyalty plays in the moral issues that soldiers encounter in their work. In the next section we will describe what loyalty is, distinguishing two different forms of loyalty: loyalty to one's own group and loyalty to a principle or profession. The subsequent section illustrates the argument by addressing a specific loyalty problem: dual loyalty. The last section before the discussion focuses on the question of how loyal it really is to expect loyalty from your colleagues.

2 What Is Loyalty?

The example of Hueting shows that loyalty features prominently in the military profession – as in fact it does in all professions in which group formation and socialisation play a major role. But what is loyalty? The fact that this question is not easy to answer is mainly because the term loyalty can mean different – and sometimes conflicting – things. The form of loyalty we saw above among Netherlands Indies veterans is loyalty to one's own group. In this particular case that group consisted of fellow soldiers, but the group may also consist of one's own family, tribe or people. Loyalty to such a group means that the interests of that group take precedence over the interests of others, even if they actually should not (Ewin 1992, p. 406). The latter occurs, for example, if someone protects fellow group members when they commit a serious error. The form of loyalty motivating Hueting was loyalty to a principle – which has a much wider scope. This broader form of loyalty plays a much more limited role in most armed forces than that of loyalty to colleagues and the organisation.

The fact that different people interpret the term in different ways means that they have different ideas about what loyalty requires from someone – Hueting undoubtedly felt that he was also being loyal in his own way. Many morally difficult situations arise because loyalty to the group makes demands that are often at odds with the requirements of loyalty to a principle. Incidentally, most ethicists value loyalty to principles more highly: in their view, group loyalty presupposes the suspension of a person's own independent judgment (Ewin 1992, p. 412). For this reason, loyalty is sometimes referred to as a 'grey' (Miller 2000, p. 8) or instrumental (Coleman 2009, p. 110) virtue: whether it really is a commendable quality depends on what one is loyal to and what the consequences are. So if loyalty is not by definition a virtue, then we should also question whether an absence of loyalty is a vice. It makes quite a difference whether someone is loyal to his or her group or organisation, or to a profession or principle. It could be argued that Hueting and other whistleblowers are loyal to their profession or to their principles, but not to their group and organisation, or at least not at any cost.

Furthermore, there is another reason why applying the term 'virtue' to loyalty is questionable: it might be better to refer to loyalty as a value. Although both concepts are sometimes used interchangeably, they are in fact different. A value is an ideal, a principle or an inner conviction (see Chapter 1). It is 'something' that you strive for, but that lies outside yourself. A virtue is a valuable character trait that you acquire through practice and have entirely internalised. By way of an example: equality is a value, courage is a virtue. Confusingly though, the concepts of virtue and value at times approximate each other very closely, because some traits that we consider as moral virtues also function as values. Justice is a good example: it is both a virtue and a value. We appreciate it as a personal trait, but also see its importance in society. Loyalty may also be an example: we appreciate it as a trait, but may also feel that it should play a role in our society or the organisation we work for. We will return to this later. Incidentally, most armed forces refer to virtues as well as values when discussing matters like bravery, discipline and loyalty, as if the terms were interchangeable. The term virtue fits best with what they seem to envisage: qualities that can be acquired through training and education. Then the question is, of course, what those qualities should be.

Featuring prominently on the virtues list of most armed forces are virtues that promote military effectiveness, such as bravery, obedience and loyalty. To an extent, these virtues are functional and mainly focused on the organisation's and the mission's interests. That is the reason why soldiers like seeing those virtues in fellow soldiers. They are not necessarily virtues requiring soldiers to have consideration for people outside the organisation, such as the local population in a deployment area. This has always been the case; however, it is remarkable that in recent years some armed forces have tended to place a greater, rather than a lesser, emphasis on martial identity. An example in the English-speaking world is the term 'warrior' which is supplanting the term 'soldier'. Ironically, this may be a reaction to the increasingly frequent deployment of military personnel to new, more humanitarian tasks that leave less room for being a 'warrior' (see also Robinson 2007).

The Netherlands armed forces do not in fact have such a concrete list of virtues, but what they do have is a code of conduct. This code of conduct was renewed in 2018 and now refers to the values of 'connectedness', 'safety', 'trust' and 'responsibility'. A noteworthy feature of this code of conduct is that it mainly aims to regulate the interaction between military personnel themselves. So ultimately, this code of conduct is oriented more towards protecting military personnel against bullying, sexual harassment and discrimination by colleagues than towards protecting, for example, the local population in a deployment area. This inward focus of many of the virtues lists and of the Dutch code of conduct is in line with armed forces' tendency to set the greatest store by group loyalty.

A similar phenomenon can be witnessed when soldiers take an oath or affirmation upon their enlistment or commission, in which they swear or affirm allegiance to the constitution, their country and/or the head of state. The 'client' of the military professional is not, or at least not initially, the civilian in the deployment area. For Dutch military personnel this oath or affirmation reads: 'I swear (affirm) that I will bear allegiance to the King/Queen, that I will obey the laws and that I will submit to military discipline. So help me God (I affirm this)' (Article 126a of the General Military Civil Servant Regulations).

In addition to the military oath or affirmation and the code of conduct, the various units within the Netherlands armed forces have their own core values. These core values partly correspond to the 'virtues lists' of other countries. The Commando Corps of the Royal Netherlands Army, for example, mentions bravery, leadership, faithfulness, honour and pride. In that context, faithfulness is understood to mean: faithfulness to your mission, faithfulness to your comrades, faithfulness to the Corps and faithfulness to yourself.[5] This corresponds to loyalty as described above. The Marine Corps of the Royal Netherlands Navy mentions connectedness, strength and dedication, where connectedness is defined as 'the most powerful weapon to overcome danger, fear and stress during operations. This special connection is based on loyalty and respect for each other and each other's opinions.'[6] Here, too, loyalty features strongly. In

---

5   See https://www.korpscommandotroepen.nl/korps/kernwaarden-van-het-korps-commando troepen/.

6   See http://de-mariniers.korpsmariniers.com/de-marinier/korpswaarden/.

brief, when soldiers talk about loyalty within the armed forces, they are talking mainly about faithfulness. They are faithful to the political leadership, to the organisation, to their mission and, most of all, to each other. This is reflected in the so-called 'can-do' mentality of soldiers. 'To keep going where others give up' is a motto soldiers often use, and frequently live up to as well.

Sometimes that faithfulness to, and protection of, each other also comes into play when unacceptable events take place. In Somalia in 1993 a number of Canadian airborne troops, who are known for their strong group loyalty and had previously been in the news because of their hazing rituals (Winslow 1999), beat to death a Somali teenager, Shidane Arone, who had slipped into the camp. A reconstruction in court revealed that at least sixteen colleagues must have witnessed or heard this, but not a single one had intervened. In a move not dissimilar to My Lai, the Canadian Department of National Defence covered up the incident. When the incident was eventually revealed, Canada disbanded the unit (Winslow 1999). A more recent example is that of Joe Darby, the US Military Police sergeant who in 2004 handed over two CDs with the now famous photos of abuses in Abu Ghraib prison to the authorities. By doing so, he was denouncing an obvious abuse, but at the same time his actions resulted in lengthy prison sentences for some of his colleagues. Integrity, another frequently cited military virtue, conflicts with loyalty to colleagues in this case: integrity and loyalty are two different things which set requirements that are sometimes incompatible. For Darby, acting with integrity, in the sense of doing what your personal values and moral standards tell you to do (and, in that sense, integrity resembles loyalty to principles), carried more weight than loyalty to his military colleagues. It should be noted in this respect that integrity features as often on the list of virtues of various countries' armed forces as do bravery and loyalty. Although the US Army also mentions integrity as one of its seven values, Darby did not fare well as a result of his action. Despite Darby having been assured of anonymity in exchange for his cooperation, his name was disclosed at a press conference by Secretary of Defense Donald Rumsfeld. Many colleagues were so resentful about Darby's alleged disloyalty that the US military authorities had to move Darby and his wife to a secret location. In that respect, not much has changed since the times of Hueting. Rumsfeld went on to write to Darby asking him to stop saying that he, Rumsfeld, had revealed Darby's name. Darby did not comply with this request (Rather 2012). Lastly, a 2006 report on the mental state of US soldiers in the same Iraq war showed that only 55 percent of soldiers were prepared to report a colleague who had injured or killed an innocent non-combatant. At 40 percent, this percentage is (even) lower for marines (Mental Health Advisory Team IV 2006). It seems

LOYALTY

that the closer-knit the unit, the more difficult it is for unit members to signal obvious abuses.

3 Dual Loyalty

Thompson, Hueting and Darby put principles before colleagues and organisation. Although the situation in which they found themselves seems exceptional, there are professions in which conflicts between group loyalty and principles are sometimes inevitable. Examples may help to clarify this, while at the same time shedding light on the unique nature of the military profession. As we have seen, military personnel take an oath (or affirmation), the Defence organisation has a code of conduct and various services and units have their own core values. Oaths, codes of conduct and core values communicate clearly what an organisation or unit considers important. And that appears to be mainly the interest of the organisation and colleagues. In that sense, the military profession is rather different from the medical profession: the medical oath (and medical ethics in general) is outwardly oriented and focuses on the patient. The interests of colleagues and the hospital are subordinate to this. *Military* medical personnel are in a special position in that they take two oaths: the medical oath and the military oath. Sometimes this will place military medical personnel in a difficult position in which two forms of loyalty conflict. We regularly see instances where medical and military ethics are difficult to reconcile. For example, there is the case in Guantanamo Bay where medical personnel failed to intervene during an unlawful interrogation which they attended to advise the commanders. As a result of hours-long interrogations, prisoners were at risk of sustaining permanent injury due to lack of sleep, among other things. They failed to make reports of this and even cooperated in the abuse of detainees (Clark 2006). Medical personnel in Guantanamo Bay were loyal to their colleagues and to their country (provision of information), but not to medical ethics. Again we see that different loyalties may clash. We also see this dual loyalty among Dutch military medical personnel. They are regularly confronted with dilemmas in deployment areas, albeit of a different kind from the example of Guantanamo Bay.

Since 2002, Dutch military personnel have assisted in improving security in Afghanistan, particularly in Uruzgan province and later in Kunduz. An example of a dilemma in this context: a vehicle on patrol hits an improvised explosive device, and a general military nurse in a vehicle behind it sees this happen. Several people are injured and the military nurse faces a difficult choice: who should she help first, a badly wounded insurgent, a local bystander, or a slightly injured colleague? A Dutch general military nurse deployed to Afghanistan stated that although the rules prescribe that a more severely wounded Taliban warrior should be cared for before a less severely injured colleague, this nurse would still choose to help the colleague first in such as case.

> I myself experienced having two wounded, one of whom was Taliban and the other an ISAF soldier. Officially, you have to go for the most seriously injured, but I didn't do that, I just went for the ISAF soldier. That was something to keep quiet about afterwards, because otherwise I'd be held to account for it. But at that moment, I really didn't care what the rules were; you become tough out there and it's a totally different way of life than you're used to here. When you see your mates getting shot and people getting killed around you, you start to feel differently about things.
> MEERBACH 2009

Military medical personnel also regularly face dilemmas about providing medicines intended for military personnel which would greatly help local civilians asking for help. We saw a poignant example of this dilemma in Chapter 2. Military ethics, which is inherently partial and puts the interests of colleagues before those of outsiders, often prevails over medical ethics, which is preeminently impartial. The fact that soldiers are often so loyal towards each other and towards the organisation is partly due to the fact that soldiers are so thoroughly socialised in their organisation. Soldiers are predominantly trained in-house, while professionals in other sectors (such as the medical sector) obtain most of their professional knowledge and skills outside their working environment. Conflicts of loyalty such as those described are also seen in other professionals in the armed forces, such as controllers, advisers and lawyers, but also in personnel of the Royal Netherlands Marechaussee in so far as they are charged with police tasks within the armed forces.

4   May Loyalty Always Be Expected?

The penultimate section showed that loyalty raises quite a few moral issues. We should therefore ask ourselves to what extent we may expect, or even demand, loyalty from colleagues. Should a soldier report a colleague who falls asleep during his watch, or should he keep quiet about it? To answer such questions, it is important to first address the difference between a moral dilemma and a test of your integrity. Not all difficult decisions pose a moral dilemma. As indicated in previous chapters, we speak of a moral dilemma when there is a conflict between values; the difficulty lies in determining what the right thing to do is in such a situation. When there is a dilemma, there is no single correct decision or choice. It is often a choice between two evils, and you should consider yourself lucky if it is even clear what the least bad solution is. However, some difficult choices are more a test of your own integrity than a real dilemma. In such an integrity test it is indeed clear what the right thing to do is, but under the pressure of circumstances (e.g. peer or group pressure or self-interest) some people will make the wrong choice (Coleman 2009). Loyalty is such a circumstance. To give an example: from a medical ethics point of view, military medical personnel who have to choose between colleagues and professional principles are faced with an integrity test, not a moral dilemma. It is clear what the right thing to do is; there is, at most, external pressure to act otherwise.

Soldiers faced with a loyalty issue – should I report my colleague who has behaved incorrectly to my superior? – will often perceive this as a moral dilemma, in which loyalty and the importance of doing the right thing clash. But strictly speaking, as said before, this is a test of your integrity: taken at face value, the loyalty a person feels for his or her own group is nothing more or less than a circumstance that can persuade a person to do the wrong thing (Coleman 2009). This also means that someone who reports misconduct by a colleague is not disloyal; it is the misbehaving colleague who expects others to look the other way who is disloyal. Seen in this light, loyalty issues are nothing more than an illustration of the old adage that knowing the right thing to do is ultimately not the same as doing it. That, however, is perhaps an oversimplification: for it may underestimate the extent to which loyalty in a military organisation not only implies outside pressure, but also a value felt from within (see also Olsthoorn 2019). What if loyalty to colleagues is so important to a person that it represents a value to him or her? Many soldiers will certainly see loyalty this way. That explains at least why soldiers do perceive a dilemma. Again, an example may shed some light on the matter.

The famous West Point Honor Code states that 'A cadet will not lie, cheat, steal, or tolerate those who do'. This motto means not only that a cadet may not lie, cheat or steal, but also that he or she must report a colleague who does to a relevant authority, for example a superior. Particularly the latter element is sensitive. It suggests that denouncing colleagues, who may also be friends, is honourable, and not denouncing them dishonourable. This is at odds with the notion that, in practice, honour is traditionally associated with a great loyalty to one's own honour group. This tension manifested itself in West Point in 2013 when it appeared that some members of the rugby team would not be allowed to graduate on account of certain inappropriate emails they had sent; the rest of the team threatened to refuse to graduate as well if that were to happen. The team members put the unwritten code of honour of their own team before the Academy's official Honor Code (Anderson and McDonald 2019).

Similar mechanisms can be seen in the Netherlands. With regard to the Netherlands Defence Academy, the Central Defence Integrity Organisation wrote that 'the great value that is attached to loyalty, group formation and comradeship and the intensive formation that military personnel undergo together' can 'sow the seeds for a military practice in which there is an excessive inward focus' (2014, p. 10). The main reason given by cadets and midshipmen for an unwillingness to report incidents is 'the idea that it is not in keeping with comradeship, that it is disloyal' (2014, p. 18). Military training reinforces this, being sometimes aimed more at teaching group loyalty than at cultivating autonomous individuals (see also Jansen 2019). Military personnel usually identify mainly with the small group of colleagues with whom they spend most of their time. Interestingly, group loyalty here requires something different (i.e. not reporting) than loyalty to the organisation.

With regard to the Defence organisation as a whole, the aforementioned report on social safety within the Dutch Defence organization similarly held that loyalty to the group can reduce the willingness to report incidents (Giebels, Van Oostrum and Van den Bos 2018, p. 65). According to the report, the organisational culture with its emphasis on loyalty is in any case an important cause of a lack of social safety: 'Loyalty is a great good and important for conducting operations, particularly during deployment. The downside of this essentially strong point of the organisation, however, is that there is a tendency to protect members of one's own group, even in the case of unacceptable behaviour, and to treat colleagues who fall outside the group unfavourably' (2018, p. 7). The fate of Hueting and Darby illustrate where this can lead to. Helicopter pilot Thompson had good reason to name 'negative peer pressure' as an explanation for My Lai (Thompson 2003). Notably, the report nevertheless mentions loyalty to the group as an element of the job profile required for working at the Defence organisation (2018, p. 65).

The committee that authored the report itself acknowledges that it is not the first to put its finger on the problem by pointing out the role of loyalty in abuses within the Defence organisation, but believes that that same loyalty is also the main reason why so little has changed after a series of reports on the subject: 'Many reports have already been written about cultural aspects in the Defence organisation. So how come that we are not able to change? Maybe it is precisely because of the loyalty of employees to their organisation and to their duty. This is both a strength and a weakness' (Giebels, Van Oostrum and Van den Bos 2018, p. 59).

LOYALTY   51

5   Discussion

When soldiers talk about loyalty, they usually mean loyalty to what is closest to them; faithfulness to colleagues and faithfulness to the organisation. Loyalty to a principle has a broader scope, but plays has a smaller role within the armed forces. Although this emphasis on loyalty to colleagues in the armed forces is understandable for several reasons, it increases both the likelihood of incidents and the likelihood of those incidents being covered up. This brings us to the question of whether armed forces should actually place so much emphasis on loyalty to the group and the organisation in education and training. Or more specifically: should they perhaps sometimes place a greater emphasis on loyalty to principles than on loyalty to the group? The report on social safety within the Dutch Defence organization, mentioned several times already, sees an important role for the education of military personnel in this field. Education is now still part of the problem, because it contributes to the strong group culture in which loyalty to colleagues plays such a major role (Giebels, Van Oostrum and Van den Bos 2018, p. 61). At the same time, education is also where the solution begins, because that is where soldiers at the start of their careers can learn that there are higher loyalties than those to the group, such as loyalty to one's own professional ethics.[7] As My Lai hero Hugh Thompson put it when talking about his colleagues on the ground who were killing innocent civilians: 'These were not soldiers. They were not military people' (2003, p. 18).

Literature

Anderson, J.M., McDonald, K.W. (2019). *Pursuing the Honorable: Reawakening Honor in the Modern Military*, Lanham, MD: Lexington Books.

Angers, T. (2014). *The Forgotten Hero of My Lai: The Hugh Thompson Story*. Lafayette: Acadian House.

Central Defence Integrity Organisation (2014). *Integriteit bij de opleiding en vorming van adelborsten en cadetten aan de Nederlandse Defensie Academie duiding van risico's, perspectief op verbetering*. Support Command.

---

7   In a recent manual on military ethics, for example, we read that '(...) being a member of the military profession (...) means adhering to the ethical standards of that profession (...) rather than simply complying with the law. Thus, in any situation where law and ethics set different standards, a member of the military profession will follow the higher standard, inevitably the one required by ethics (...)' (Coleman 2013, p. 268).

Clark, P.A. (2006). 'Medical Ethics at Guantanamo Bay and Abu Ghraib: The Problem of Dual Loyalty.' *The Journal of Law, Medicine & Ethics 34*(3) pp. 570–580.

Coleman, S. (2009). 'The Problems of Duty and Loyalty.' *Journal of Military Ethics 8*(2).

Coleman, S. (2013). *Military Ethics*. Oxford: Oxford University Press.

Defence Leadership Vision (2014). Defence Leadership Centre of Expertise.

Ewin, R.E. (1992). 'Loyalty and Virtues.' *Philosophical Quarterly, 42*(169), pp. 403–419.

Giebels, E., Oostrum, F. van, & Bos, K. van den (2018). *Commissie Sociaal Veilige Werkomgeving Defensie, eindrapportage: Onderzoek naar een sociaal veilige werkomgeving bij Defensie.*

Jansen, M. (2019). *Educating for Military Realities*. Nijmegen: Radboud University.

Kidder, Rushworth M. (2005). *Moral Courage*. New York: Harper Collins.

McDermott, T. and Hart, S. (2017). 'Armouring Against Atrocity: Developing Ethical Strength in Small Military Units.' In: P. Olsthoorn (ed.), *Military Ethics and Leadership*, pp. 16–55. Leiden: Brill.

Meerbach, C.M.C. (2009). *Morele Professionaliteit van Algemeen Militair Verpleegkundigen in Hedendaagse Operaties*, Breda: Netherlands Defence Academy.

Mental Health Advisory Team IV (2006), *Operation Iraqi Freedom 05–07 Final Report.* Washington, D.C.: Office of the Surgeon, Multinational Force-Iraq and Office of the Surgeon General, United States Army Medical Command.

Miles, S.H. (2006). *Oath Betrayed: Torture, Medical Complicity, and the War on Terror.* New York: Random House.

Miller, I. (2000). *The Mystery of Courage*. Cambridge: Harvard University Press.

Olsthoorn, P. (2019). 'Dual Loyalty in Military Medical Ethics: A Moral Dilemma or a Test of Integrity?' *Journal of the Royal Army Medical Corps, 165*(4), pp. 282–283.

Rather, D. (2012). *Rather Outspoken: My Life in the News*. New York: Grand Central.

Robinson, P. (2007). 'The Way of the Warrior.' *Spectator*, June 13.

Thompson, H. (2003). *Moral Courage in Combat: The My Lai Story*. Annapolis: United States Naval Academy. Consulted on: https://www.usna.edu/Ethics/_files/documents/Thompson-Pg1-28_Final.pdf.

Verweij, D.E.M. (2009). 'Militaire Ethiek.' In: R. Moelker, J. Noll and M. de Weger (eds.), *Krijgsmacht en samenleving. Over de inzet van een geweldsinstrument: bestuurlijke, politieke en veiligheidsaspecten*. Amsterdam: Boom.

Winslow, D. (1999). 'Rites of Passage and Group Bonding in the Canadian Airborne.' *Armed Forces and Society 25*(3), p. 429–57.

CHAPTER 5

Moral Injury

The Psychological Impact of Morally Critical Situations

Tine Molendijk

1 Introduction

Military practice is an area of moral tension, a field where questions about right and wrong come up all the time and different values can clash with one another, giving rise to dilemmas and other moral challenges. Some moral challenges can do so much violence to one's own moral beliefs that they cause psychological damage. A soldier can develop a moral injury.

At the same time, for many soldiers, day-to-day practice could hardly feel farther removed from being 'an area of moral tension' and mentioning a term like this in the workplace may well be met with laughter by colleagues. Many soldiers will point out that to them their work is just as morally complicated as any other type of work. 'You know well what is right and wrong,' one might say with a shrug. And another might say: 'You just have to use your common sense'.

To some extent this indifference may lie in the military can-do mentality, which focuses on being concrete and solving problems, and not on doubts and using 'woolly' language such as 'area of moral tension'. Partly it will also lie in the fact that terms like these often evoke highly exceptional, Hollywood-like images, for example of snipers who must decide whether or not to kill a child. Then there is the prevailing idea that only direct confrontations with physical danger can lead to serious psychological problems, so that stress caused by other situations will easily be seen in terms of a personal shortcoming.

Upon closer examination, however, the opposite turns out to be true. Morally critical events, be they not so extreme as in Hollywood films, are relatively common in military practice, and soldiers are relatively often caught off guard by situations in which deciding what is the right thing to do is not so clear at all. In contemporary missions, soldiers often have to operate among and with the local population, while they usually have no possibilities to do anything about local poverty, disease and suffering and, moreover, it is not always clear to what extent the opponent is really a malicious enemy. When these complexities find expression in a concrete critical situation, feelings of guilt, shame or betrayal may arise. Just as shrapnel can cause a flesh wound,

© KONINKLIJKE BRILL NV, LEIDEN, 2022 | DOI:10.1163/9789004512474_006

and just as a life-threatening event can disrupt a person's stress regulation, the witnessing, performing or enduring of acts that do violence to one's own moral beliefs can lead to moral injury.

This moral injury is the subject of this chapter. First, the concept of moral injury is discussed and the distinction between post-traumatic stress disorder (PTSD) and moral injury is clarified. Subsequently, the nature and potential causes of moral injury, including political and societal aspects, will be addressed. Finally, possible answers to the problem are considered. Before all this, however, the stories of two soldiers, Bob and Gio (not their real names), are told to sketch a picture of what moral injury can mean in practice. These stories are the result of interviews conducted as part of Tine Molendijk's research into moral injury (Molendijk 2021). The stories have been somewhat generalised, to protect the anonymity of the service members involved and to make clear that the broader themes in their stories are also applicable to future missions.

2 Gio's Story: 'A Good Soldier, But Not a Good Person'

Soon after entering the service, Gio felt 'right at home in the army'. He had always been a doer and loved the action and the spirit of brotherhood existing in the armed forces. Although making the world a better place was not his primary goal, he did like the idea of 'being able to help people'. He did perceive his first deployments like that, or at least as valuable adventures in which he could put his training into practice. But this was not the case with his third deployment; that one turned out to be different.

During that mission, Gio and his unit stayed in a 'home compound' for some time. Every night in the dark he heard a boy of about fourteen crying. The boy was a *bacha*, known among Western troops as a *chai boy*. As discussed earlier in Chapter 3, this means a boy who is owned by a rich, influential man and who must provide entertainment and sexual services on demand (see also Schut & Van Baarle 2017). During the day Gio often saw the boy looking at him. He is begging for help, Gio would think to himself. 'But you weren't allowed to do anything. You couldn't take him with you, or something like that. So you'd sit there at your guard post at night and you'd hear that kid crying,' he remembers. 'It was heart-rending. And you felt like total shit.' But, tragically, that was not all. A few days later Gio heard 'that the kid had shot himself through the head with an AK'. He still lies awake at night, and torments himself, thinking: if only I had done something. He is also tormented by the fact that he was not *allowed* to do anything. It was a local custom among powerful men, and cooperation

MORAL INJURY

with them was badly needed for the success of the mission. 'That kind of ambiguity gnaws at you,' says Gio. He had acted 'as a good soldier' but did not feel like 'a good person'.

After coming home Gio developed deep feelings of guilt. He started 'drinking a lot and driving fast' in order not to have to think of the things that gnawed at him. While driving he often thought: all I have to do is yank the steering wheel and it's all over. He was being self-destructive, he later realised, because he subconsciously felt he deserved it. He felt very strongly 'that I still had to be punished somehow for what had happened'. For a while, he had even entertained the paranoid idea that his mother wanted to poison him. At the same time he felt betrayed and abandoned by the military organisation and politicians. He had been deployed on a mission in which there was cooperation with child-abusing warlords, whereas nobody there had told him that having chai boys 'was also simply illegal under local law'. In addition, he and his colleagues had to do a great deal of fighting in this mission, with many civilian casualties, while the mission was 'sold as a reconstruction mission back home'. Gio experienced ambivalence regarding all these points, which he was unable to mentally resolve. He is doing better now, but it was a long struggle for him.

3   Bob's Story: 'What Am I Doing Here?'

Bob was deployed as a peacekeeper on a UN mission and was looking forward to putting his training into practice. It soon became clear, however, that this would be entirely impossible during this deployment. In this mission, UN troops had far too few resources and authorisations to carry out their tasks, and the various warring factions seemed quite unfazed by their presence. 'In practice, there was no peace to keep,' Bob would later say. The warring parties would even intentionally fire over Bob's and his colleagues' heads on a regular basis in order to harass and intimidate them. Increasingly often he began to think: what am I doing here?

One night, while on guard at a village, through his binoculars Bob saw two local fighters approaching. They fired a mortar at one of the houses, and two men came running outside. One was shot directly in the neck – 'his throat simply came off' – the other was shot dead while trying to crawl towards the first one. 'We'll shoot them to bits,' Bob told his colleagues, but their commander would not let them do anything. There were too few of them and they would have no chance if things escalated. So they did nothing. One of the fighters waved at Bob triumphantly, which he found deeply humiliating. Not long afterwards, they heard gunshots again, this time from the other party, but again the soldiers could do nothing but take cover and wait. And this is how Bob experienced his entire deployment: hiding and waiting, powerless, not being able or allowed to do anything about the many incidents that followed.

Back in the Netherlands Bob began drinking and partying a lot. He kept his experiences to himself, fearful that people would not believe him and would confront him with difficult questions and accusations, because by then heated debates about his mission had begun in the media. His behaviour towards colleagues became volatile, and he also started acting aggressively outside work. Once he had to appear in court, 'for an act of stupidity'. In the meantime, he became more and more doubtful about his deployment: 'For a long time I managed to hold on, like, I did my best. But I began to doubt myself more and more.' Eventually he collapsed.

After prolonged treatment and a lot of talking about his experiences with his girlfriend, Bob is doing better again. He is proud of himself. He is proud of the fact that as a result of his deployment experiences he is able to see things in perspective and that he knows what is really important in life. Moreover, he is proud of his deployment itself, of what he was able to do there. At the same time, he still feels deeply guilty about all the things he was unable to achieve there and furious that he and his colleagues were sent on such an 'impossible mission'. To him, the blue UN beret he had to wear during the mission symbolises all that. He has never worn that beret again, but has not thrown it away either. After all: 'You can't throw away your past.'

4 Post-traumatic Stress Disorder and Moral Injury

For many, the stories of Gio and Bob will bring to mind the term post-traumatic stress disorder. This is today's most used term for psychological problems among soldiers, so well known that even the acronym PTSD is common usage. But is it actually the most appropriate term for experiences like those of Gio and Bob? It is of course impossible to base a diagnosis on a short story, but a few points can be noted. According to the most recent official definition, PTSD may develop after experience of or directly or indirectly witnessing 'actual or threatened death, serious injury, or sexual violence' (DSM-5 2013: 271), and according to most PTSD models fear responses are at the heart of post-traumatic stress (DePrince & Freyd 2002). Although the stories of both Gio and Bob indeed contain instances of witnessing violence, they also appear to be different from the above-mentioned characteristics. Their stories are not so much centred on exposure to threat and fear-related responses, but rather on experiences of moral conflict and resulting feelings of guilt, shame and anger.

And that is precisely what the concept of moral injury is about. Although PTSD and moral injury are not mutually exclusive and partly overlap in practice, their focus is different. There is as yet no agreement on the precise definition of moral injury – the concept is relatively new – but current research on the subject usually defines moral injury as the psychological, biological and social impact of a transgression of deeply held beliefs and expectations, of which the morally injured person may have been the victim, the witness or the perpetrator, at least in his/her own eyes (see Frankfurt & Frazier 2016; Litz et al. 2009; Shay 2014). Unlike in the case of PTSD, in moral injury the emphasis is specifically on the moral dimension of shocking events.

A first conceptual model of moral injury was introduced in 2009 (Litz et al. 2009). Since then, the concept has rapidly gained currency in research, treatment and policy aimed at soldiers and veterans. This is not surprising considering the statistics. Take, for example, a recent survey among US service members. More than 10 percent of them reported having been involved in moral transgressions and more than 25 percent had witnessed moral transgressions committed by others (Wisco et al. 2017). In another survey more than 25 percent of the subjects indicated that they had experienced 'ethical situations' in which they did not know how to respond (MHAT-V 2008). Regarding the impact of such events, several studies show percentages between 5 and 25 of service personnel suffering from feelings of guilt, shame or anger resulting from their deployment experiences (Bryan et al. 2016; Currier et al. 2015; Wisco et al. 2017).

According to the literature on the subject, potentially morally injurious events include the injury and killing of others, the inability to prevent suffering among colleagues or civilians, and omissions by a leader or other authority (Griffin et al. 2019). This enumeration shows that moral injury is not the preserve of personnel deployed on combat missions, but may also occur in peacekeeping operations. A study among Dutch veterans of peacekeeping missions confirms this. Of the peacekeepers surveyed, a quarter admitted to feelings of guilt about the deployment, and at least a third of this quarter said that this guilt had caused substantial suffering (Rietveld 2015). Furthermore, it is plausible that professional groups such as medical and police personnel are also at risk of developing moral injury. In fact, considering that life has bigger and smaller moral dilemmas in store for all of us, it seems that every person could, to a greater or lesser degree, become morally injured.

It would certainly be wrong to think that in PTSD research the moral dimension of trauma has gone unnoticed all this time. Indeed, when the concept of PTSD gained prominence in the 1980s in connection with the Vietnam War, a great deal of attention was paid to both guilt and anger directed towards military and political leaders (see, for example, Lifton 1973). And although these moral emotions became underexposed in the decades that followed, they are back in the picture nowadays. The most recent definition of PTSD even explicitly mentions as a possible symptom of PTSD: 'persistent, distorted cognitions about the cause or consequences of the traumatic event(s) that lead the individual to blame himself/herself or others.' (DSM-5 2013: 272). But, as this description also suggests, in current PTSD research guilt and blame are mainly treated as resulting from irrational thoughts, i.e. as misplaced emotions. By contrast, the literature on moral injury explicitly goes against such an approach, and the term 'injury' instead of 'disorder' is no coincidence. Moral injury emphasises that moral considerations and judgments should be taken seriously, and that feelings of guilt, shame and/or betrayal should therefore be considered potentially 'appropriate' emotions (see also Table 5.1). Indeed, it is moral considerations and emotions that make a person human.

TABLE 5.1   Current PTSD models and Moral Injury model

	Current PTSD models	Moral Injury model
Cause	(Life-)threatening situation	Situation that transgresses moral beliefs and expectations
	The perception of safety is harmed	*The perception of a just world is harmed*
The individual's role in the situation	Victim or witness	Victim, witness or (in his/her own eyes) person responsible
Central emotions	Fear-related emotions, such as feelings of danger and threat	Moral emotions, such as feelings of guilt, shame and betrayal
Approach to possible judgment of oneself or others	Misplaced, result of 'distorted cognitions', deresponsibilisation needed	Appropriate, (self-) forgiveness needed where applicable

5   Individual Dimensions of Moral Injury

In the armed forces personnel often refer to a moral code or compass when speaking about ethics. Although to an extent these are suitable metaphors for a person's values and moral standards, it is important to realise that they never form a neatly harmonious unity, but always a complex, even 'messy' whole (Tessman 2014; Zigon 2008). This applies to all people, including, and perhaps even specifically, to soldiers. Like all people, soldiers are part of a family, a circle of friends, various subcultures and society as a whole, and all these social spheres have their own specific values and moral standards that are not necessarily neatly in tune with one another. In addition, soldiers belong to a military community, with values and standards that may be at odds with those of society and, moreover, may conflict with each other: soldiers must be loyal to their 'brotherhood' but also guarantee the safety of civilians, and in doing so they must at all times comply with their political mission (see also Chapters 1 and 4). Moreover, they must try to manage all these values and moral standards in high-risk environments, as potential targets, witnesses and performers of violence (Baarda & Verweij 2006).

Given these complexities, it is not surprising that soldiers can experience situations that lead to feelings of guilt, shame or betrayal. Partly because of the complexities mentioned above, these situations themselves are often characterised by conflict. We see this, for example, in the stories of Gio and Bob and their experience of a conflict between being a good soldier and a good person. It also applies to the moral dilemma discussed in Chapter 2 and the cases of moral disengagement described in Chapter 3, in which service members transgressed moral boundaries that they would not have transgressed under normal circumstances, because these boundaries were less clear-cut at that moment. These types of experiences are more complex than the unambiguous feeling that a moral code has *undeniably* been violated, or that one's moral compass has *undeniably* been deviated from. Such experiences engender feelings of conflict.

Such experiences may cause morally injured soldiers to suffer feelings of guilt and shame as well as anger towards others, or even towards the world at large. In addition, soldiers can become morally disoriented, and become profoundly confused about matters that previously seemed to be just common sense. All kinds of questions can arise, such as: 'Was I a good soldier, and is a good soldier also a good person?', 'Do my feelings of guilt make me a good or a bad person?', 'How can you possibly do good in situations that force you to choose between two evils?' and 'What do good and bad mean anyway?' These are ethical questions that under normal circumstances are asked mainly by ethicists and moral psychologists, but when they come up as a result of moral injury, they are no longer abstract scientific questions, but deeply personal and often very painful ones. They can make morally injured soldiers lose confidence in the goodness of both themselves and the world surrounding them, and even in the idea of goodness itself (for a more extensive discussion of this point, see Molendijk 2018b).

6 Political and Societal Dimensions of Moral Injury

As mentioned above, morally injured soldiers may also develop anger, for example towards politics and society (for an elaboration of this section, see Molendijk 2018a and Molendijk 2019). Soldiers are instruments of the state, who do their work in the name of society, as noted in Chapter 1. Therefore, as a feature specific to military practice, questions about good and evil do not remain in the soldier's private sphere, but are explicitly raised and discussed in the political and societal domains. The missions in Vietnam, Rwanda and Bosnia are notorious examples of how failures in political decision-making can have disastrous consequences. Logically, they also offer examples of the heated public debates that may follow. Although these examples are extreme, they are not in principle unique. Many soldiers deployed on a great many different missions, like Gio and Bob, have stories to tell about how political and public practices created difficult situations during and after their deployment.

To start with the impact of political practices: if soldiers experience morally injurious events during their deployment and if they perceive these to have been related to avoidable political failure, this may cause a strong sense of political betrayal. That feeling can in turn manifest itself in distrust, anger, and, more concretely, in seeking satisfaction. For example, hundreds of Dutch Bosnia veterans have recently sued the government for the emotional damage they have incurred as a result of their deployment. Formally, their collective claim was for financial compensation, but many veterans were above all seeking symbolic compensation in the form of recognition. They saw a lawsuit, as one of them put it, 'as the only way to make the state pay for its failure' (Molendijk 2021). When the government announced it was to undertake a large-scale investigation of the healthcare needs of Bosnia veterans, they consequently dropped their collective financial claim.

Where exactly do such profound feelings of betrayal and this need for satisfaction and recognition come from? It starts with the fact that the relationship between the soldier and the state is one of dependency. This is a relationship in which the stakes are significant. They concern the physical and mental well-being of soldiers, and even their lives. In order to do their job properly, soldiers must therefore trust that they are in good hands with their own government, or at least not in the wrong hands. If this relationship of dependency and trust is damaged, the soldier may experience this is as violation of a vital moral relationship. This explains the feeling of betrayal and the need for satisfaction. This betrayal can be felt in relation to the state and the government, and also in relation to the organisation or, even more specifically, the commander (see also Chapter 1 regarding the importance of 'recognition').

In addition to betrayal by the political leadership or the organisation, military personnel may experience misrecognition by society. This perceived misrecognition is not primarily, or at least not exclusively, about a lack of appreciation. Of course, soldiers are affected when the media report negatively on how they behaved on a mission, especially if their immediate environment starts to believe they acted culpably. But heroic images and stories in which soldiers are portrayed as trauma victims are often also problematic for soldiers, because soldiers who have acted against their own values simply do not tend to feel heroic or worthy of pity. The societal misrecognition that soldiers can perceive is mainly about the feeling that their own deployment experiences become oversimplified and contorted in public opinion, and that they themselves are transformed into caricatures such as 'perpetrator', 'hero' or 'victim'. In this sense, misrecognition therefore means that their experiences are reduced to oversimplifications and that they are not viewed as human beings.

This simplification is the reason why misrecognition can be called morally injurious: injustice is being done to one's experience. And particularly when a person struggles with shocking events, that person will likely feel a need for recognition by others, even more so when the events are about injustice. Perceived misrecognition may therefore also lead to great anger, alienation and self-isolation. In addition, a mismatch with public opinion can seriously hamper soldiers in identifying and coming to terms with their experiences, because it means that existing stories in society will not provide them with the appropriate words to describe these experiences. Finally, looking at themselves through the eyes of others, soldiers may develop feelings of guilt and shame which they otherwise might not have.

7 Doing Justice to Moral Injury

How to deal with moral injury? As we have seen, moral injury can, at least in part, be considered an ethical struggle with questions of good and evil. It is for this reason that feelings of guilt, shame or anger should not be dismissed too easily as unnecessary or misplaced, but should be seen as possibly justified. Brushing them aside will not help the person in question and may even aggravate the moral injury. After all, ignoring moral emotions means not doing justice to these emotions (see also Molendijk 2018a; Shay 1994).

Of course, it may be that the soldier with moral injury places an exaggerated amount of blame on himself or others. In practice, however, a person's responsibility for a situation almost always lies somewhere between zero and full responsibility, and feelings of guilt, shame or anger therefore still have their place. At the same time, it might be useful to help morally injured soldiers in contemplating different perspectives, not for them to change their mind and judgment, but to help them get a better grip on the issue. Ultimately, it may be necessary for a morally injured soldier to seek forgiveness for himself or others. However, doing so is no simple matter. Forgiveness is a process that takes time, and only meaningful if it is sincere (Litz et al. 2015).

In order to prevent moral injury, it is first of all crucial to recognise and acknowledge the existence of the phenomenon. This implies, among other things, that training should not only focus on stressors such as exchanges of fire, but also on stress arising from confrontations with injustice, moral dilemmas and moral disengagement. Furthermore, it is important that attention be given to the moral tensions such situations may cause, and that moral transgressions that occur as a result are not readily condoned, but taken seriously. More specifically, it should be recognised that insoluble conflicts can arise between personal and professional values and between professional values and a political mission, and, additionally, that the usefulness of a deployment may seem questionable. However tempting it may be to give a more reassuring message, 'imposing' justifications and a sense of meaning will aggravate rather than heal a moral injury (see also Eidelson et al. 2011).

Knowledge of ethical concepts can be useful for learning to recognise and acknowledge morally injurious situations. Someone who does not know what exactly terms like values, moral standards and moral dilemmas mean will not be able to communicate about moral injury. This demonstrates once again the added value of ethics education. Currently, however, ethics education is largely confined to the classroom, where moral dilemmas are easily transformed into brainteasers instead of concrete situations in which emotions and stress can play an important role (Thompson & Jetly 2014). Linking ethics explicitly to field exercises, however, would make it possible to train moral resilience in a realistic manner.

Having said this, it should be acknowledged that preventing moral injury is only partly within soldiers' own control. Military practice is a collective affair. The missions on which military personnel are to be deployed, and what they should and should not do there, are determined at the political level, and debates about whether or not a mission was justified and useful are held at a broader social level. Solutions for moral injury should therefore be sought not only at the level of the individual soldier, but also at the levels of political decision-making and public debates.

At the political level, moral principles such as those of the Just War Tradition (see also Chapter 1) must be effectively included in the decision-making process regarding military intervention. These principles are embedded in international humanitarian law (including the Geneva Conventions and the Charter of the United Nations) and also in the criteria that many national governments have developed for themselves to guide decision-making on the deployment of military personnel. All this is to ensure that military units are deployed for just reasons and do their job in a just manner. Moral principles must therefore be genuinely taken into account in decision-making processes, and not just be ticked off as if they are part of a legal checklist (Verweij & Molendijk 2019). That is easier said than done. Equally important, therefore, is that government do not attempt to paint a pretty picture when communicating about military missions, but dare to be transparent and honest. The more transparent and honest the political decision-making is, the more protection it will provide against moral injury, and vice versa.

At the social level, rituals, such as the purification and reintegration rites that warriors had to undergo in earlier societies, can be valuable. Instead of making portrayals such as 'perpetrator', 'hero' or 'victim', these rituals were in fact based on nuanced ideas about the moral complexity of military practice. Take, for example, the rituals of early Christianity. Returning warriors routinely participated in various acts of atonement and cleansing so as to be purified from the moral 'pollution' of war. The warriors were not seen as sinners, but as people who had been involved in the 'justified evil' of war (Verkamp 1993). Such rituals are still extant in some societies, for example in southern African communities where they serve to release returning soldiers of the spirits of people who were killed (Granjo & Nicolini 2006).

In most western countries we no longer have institutionalised rituals of this kind. Instead, most of us are simultaneously fascinated and deeply uncomfortable when it comes to the reality of military intervention. As a result, we try to keep war and everything related to it far from us (Molendijk 2018a, 2021). However, it appears that veterans struggling with their experiences sometimes create their own rituals, for example by returning as a group to their area of deployment in order to walk a march together with the local population (Hetebrij 2010). The existence of such self-made rituals demonstrates their importance, and at the same time the current lack of them in our society. It would therefore seem useful to look at the activities that veterans themselves have initiated.

8 Conclusion

In view of the fact that military practice is by definition an area of moral tension, moral injury can never be prevented completely. More generally, we must accept that moral injury is a tragic risk of life. However, there prove to be interventions of varying effectiveness for dealing with this problem and the risk it poses. As a basic principle it has been established that recognition and acknowledgment of moral injury is very important, not only in the aftermath of deployment, but also well before it. The focus should be not only on the individual via training and therapy, but also at the levels of the military organisation, politics and society, through ethically sensitive decision-making, honest and well-nuanced communication and adequate military reintegration. In other words, it is important to *do justice* to moral injury.

In relation to this, it is important to ask whether moral injury should be seen only as a mental health issue, or also as something different or broader in scope. As a health problem it may easily end up in the domain of mental disorders, while moral injury appears to be more than only a mental disorder in the strict sense. Moral injury can also partly be understood as a painful moral-philosophical struggle, one that is not necessarily a question of misplaced emotions and thoughts, but an adequate response to moral dilemmas and to 'disorder' at the political and societal levels. More fundamentally, moral injury is about the loss of innocence in two senses: innocence within the meaning of not being guilty, and innocence within the meaning of unfamiliarity with the evil side of the world.

Literature

Baarda, T. A. van, & Verweij, D. E. M. (2006). *Military Ethics: The Dutch Approach – A Practical Guide.* Leiden: Martinus Nijhoff.

Bryan, C. J., Bryan, A. O., Anestis, M. D., Anestis, J. C., Green, B. A., Etienne, N., Morrow, C. E., & Ray-Sannerud, B. (2016). 'Measuring Moral Injury: Psychometric Properties of the Moral Injury Events Scale in Two Military Samples.' *Assessment, 23*(5), 557–570.

Currier, J. M., Holland, J. M., Drescher, K., & Foy, D. (2015). 'Initial Psychometric Evaluation of the Moral Injury Questionnaire – Military Version.' *Clinical Psychology & Psychotherapy, 22*(1), 54–63.

DePrince, A. P., & Freyd, J. J. (2002). 'The Harm of Trauma: Pathological Fear, Shattered Assumptions, or Betrayal.' In J. Kauffman (Ed.), *Loss of the Assumptive World: A Theory of Traumatic Loss* (pp. 71–82). New York: Brunner-Routledge.

DSM-5. (2013). *The Diagnostic and Statistical Manual of Mental Disorders, Fifth Edition*. Arlington, VA: American Psychiatric Association.

Eidelson, R., Pilisuk, M., & Soldz, S. (2011). 'The Dark Side of Comprehensive Soldier Fitness.' *American Psychologist, 66*(7), 643–644.

Frankfurt, S., & Frazier, P. (2016). 'A Review of Research on Moral Injury in Combat Veterans.' *Military Psychology, 28*(5), 318–330.

Granjo, P., & Nicolini, B. (2006). 'Back Home: Post-War Cleansing Rituals in Mozambique.' In *Studies in Witchcraft, Magic, War and Peace in Africa (19th and 20th Centuries)* (pp. 277–294). Lampeter: Mellemn Press.

Griffin, B. J., Purcell, N., Burkman, K., Litz, B. T., Bryan, C. J., Schmitz, M., Villierme, C., Walsh, J., & Maguen, S. (2019). 'Moral Injury: An Integrative Review.' *Journal of Traumatic Stress, 32*(3), 350–362.

Hetebrij, B. (2010). 'Terugkeerreis als Pelgrimage' [Return Journey as Pilgrimage]. *Carré, 10*, 14–17.

Lifton, R. J. (1973). *Home from the War: Learning from Vietnam Veterans*. New York: Other Press.

Litz, B. T., Lebowitz, L., Gray, M. J., & Nash, W. P. (2015). *Adaptive Disclosure: A New Treatment for Military Trauma, Loss, and Moral Injury*. New York: Guilford Publications.

Litz, B. T., Stein, N., Delaney, E., Lebowitz, L., Nash, W. P., Silva, C., & Maguen, S. (2009). 'Moral Injury and Moral Repair in War Veterans: A Preliminary Model and Intervention Strategy.' *Clinical Psychology Review, 29*(8), 695–706.

MHAT-V. (2008). *Operation Iraqi Freedom 06-08: Iraq. Operation Enduring Freedom 8: Afghanistan*. Washington, DC: Office of the Surgeon Multi-National Force: Mental Health Advisory Team. http://www.armymedicine.army.mil/reports/mhat/mhat_v/mhat-v.cfm.

Molendijk, T. (2018a). 'Moral Injury in Relation to Public Debates: The Role of Societal Misrecognition in Moral Conflict-Colored Trauma among Soldiers.' *Social Science & Medicine, 211*, 314–320.

Molendijk, T. (2018b). 'Toward an Interdisciplinary Conceptualization of Moral Injury: From Unequivocal Guilt and Anger to Moral Conflict and Disorientation.' *New Ideas in Psychology, 51*, 1–8.

Molendijk, T. (2019). 'The Role of Political Practices in Moral Injury: A Study of Afghanistan Veterans.' *Political Psychology, 40*(2), 261–275.

Molendijk, T. (2021). *Moral Injury and Soldiers in Conflict: Political Practices and Public Perceptions*. London: Routledge.

Rietveld, N. (2015). *Voorkomen is beter dan genezen. De geestelijke gezondheid van militairen en politiemensen: Risico's en beschermende factoren*. Apeldoorn: Politieacademie.

Schut, M., & Baarle, E. van (2017). 'Dancing Boys and the Moral Dilemmas of Military Missions: The Practice of Bacha Bazi in Afghanistan.' In A. B. Bah (Ed.), *International Security and Peacebuilding: Africa, the Middle East, and Europe* (pp. 77–98). Bloomington: Indiana University Press.

Shay, J. (1994). *Achilles in Vietnam: Combat Trauma and the Undoing of Character*. New York: Simon and Schuster.

Shay, J. (2014). 'Moral Injury.' *Psychoanalytic Psychology, 31*(2), 182–191.

Tessman, L. (2014). *Moral Failure: On the Impossible Demands of Morality*. Oxford: Oxford University Press.

Thompson, M. M., & Jetly, R. (2014). 'Battlefield Ethics Training: Integrating Ethical Scenarios in High-Intensity Military Field Exercises.' *European Journal of Psychotraumatology, 5*(1), 1–10.

Verkamp, B. J. (1993). *The Moral Treatment of Returning Warriors in Early Medieval and Modern Times*. Scranton: University of Scranton Press.

Verweij, D. E. M., & Molendijk, T. (2019). 'Voorkomen is beter dan genezen: Moral injury vanuit macro- en micro-perspectief' [Prevention is Better than Cure. Moral Injury from a Micro and Macro Perspective]. In M. van der Giessen, P. H. Kamphuis, E. R. Muller, U. Rosenthal, G. Valk, & E. Vermetten (Eds.), *Veteranen: Veteranen en veteranenbeleid in Nederland* [*Veterans: Veterans and Veteran Policy in the Netherlands*] (pp. 165–184). Deventer: Wolters Kluwer.

Wisco, B. E., Marx, B. P., May, C. L., Martini, B., Krystal, J. H., Southwick, S. M., & Pietrzak, R. H. (2017). 'Moral Injury in U.S. Combat Veterans: Results from the National Health and Resilience in Veterans Study.' *Depression and Anxiety, 34*(4), 340–347.

Zigon, J. (2008). *Morality: An Anthropological Perspective*. Berg.

CHAPTER 6

Ethics and Technology

Christine Boshuijzen-Van Burken

1 Introduction

In the morning of 6 April 2011, the pilot of a Predator UAV performed an air strike in the Sangin River Valley in Afghanistan. It turned out to be a catastrophic error, as he had fired on his own troops and killed a marine staff sergeant and a navy hospitalman. The pilot was operating from a distance of thousands of miles away from the scene of the incident. The empirical facts of this incident were investigated in legal and technical reports, in an attempt to find out how this could have happened and who is responsible (see Laster & Iannotta 2012). But this case also involves ethically relevant aspects regarding moral decisions in modern military operations, which we will discuss below. We will first describe the events preceding and during the incident, based on an article by Laster and Iannotta (2012), who have documented the incident extensively.

> At 08:40, the Predator crew at the Predator control station in California spotted the heat signatures of a group of three persons in the Sangin River Valley in Afghanistan. At 08:41, a burst of muzzle flashes emanated from the group. What was this group and what were these three persons up to? A critical question concerned the exact direction of the muzzle flashes. If the direction was east, towards friendly lines, they were potential insurgents trying to kill US troops. If it was west, away from friendly lines, they might be US personnel or other allies. The Predator crew and the forces in Afghanistan assumed that the muzzle flashes were coming towards friendly positions and that it therefore was an enemy group. Based on this assumption, they proceeded to carry out their tasks (culminating in the airborne attack). Only minutes earlier, ground forces had reported contact with the enemy over the Predator crew's radio link. As the Predator circled above Sangin, its ARC-210 radio received transmissions from the ground and fed them into the drone's satellite link, which relayed them to the Predator control station in California. Given the seriousness of the situation, the Predator crew furiously scanned for targets to strike with one or more of the Predator's Hellfire missiles.

© KONINKLIJKE BRILL NV, LEIDEN, 2022 | DOI:10.1163/9789004512474_007

At 08:41, the JTAC[1] in Afghanistan sent the '9-line' message containing coordinates for a strike once approved by the ground commander. The analysts at DGS[2] Indiana (DGS-IN) also saw the targets in the video feed. Based on these images, their leader chimed in with a series of online messages raising questions about their identification as enemy. This information was shared via a chat box that was not visible to everyone: a so-called 'whisper chat'.

Unfortunately the DGS-IN analysts were for various reasons unable to say with certainty where the US troops were or what the precise direction of the muzzle flashes was. As a result, they could cause confusion in their communication with the Predator crew. Due to images that were too grainy or shadowy, they were unable to determine the exact number of persons or the direction of the muzzle flashes. Because there was no voice link with the Predator crew, it proved impossible to convey this information unambiguously.

Following the deadly attack, it appeared that several members of the DGS team in Indiana had had reservations about the strike and they stated in writing that they had felt uncomfortable when the Predator started to fire.

The friendly-fire incident described above was the result of – a number of – moral decisions. Technology, such as the thermal camera that provided the images, played a central role in these decisions. Precisely because of this central role, the investigators of the incident advised that in the future any intelligence or information that could prevent friendly fire or a violation of the Law of Armed Conflict be posted in the crew's chat room. The entire crew would then be able to see and hear this intelligence and information. This was precisely not the case with the friendly-fire incident, where important information could only be reported to a few people via a whisper chat.

Air Force Major General Robert Otto agreed with the conclusions of the investigators, but also argued that the error was almost inevitable given the circumstances: 'You have to understand, the Sangin Valley is bad-guy territory (...). If you don't know where the friendlies are, it's pretty difficult for you to

---

1 Joint Tactical Air Controller. A service member who, from the ground, guides the pilot in the performance of his tasks when carrying out an attack, so that the right targets are hit with as little collateral damage as possible.

2 Distributed Ground System. A technical system by which intelligence can be analysed remotely and forwarded to, for example, ground troops.

know [what] to overturn based on what one of the supporting forces thought' (Laster and Iannotta 2012, p. 27).

As appears from the account above, the solution to such friendly-fire incidents is sought in adding more technology, i.e. by equipping the crew with voice communications on top or instead of chat communications. But merely adding more technology, for example switching from listening mode to two-way conversations, is not easy and may not be suitable for solving moral problems in decision-making on the battlefield. In Laster and Iannotta's article, Otto argues that there are technical and procedural rules that must be followed. Some of these rules require the installation of additional hardware to enable two-way communication. The right balance will also need to be struck on the issue of voice communication procedures, he adds. 'There's a point when a discussion's over. And while we always want somebody to have the ability to speak up when they fear a rule-of-engagement violation or wait a minute, there's women and children, you have to balance fighting a war by committee with a ground-force commander who is presumed to have the situational awareness and has the authority to say, we need to strike this target' (ibid).

The case example described above, including the selected passages from Laster and Iannotta's article, set the scene for this chapter on ethics and technology in modern military missions in which technology is ubiquitous. What role does technology play in taking moral decisions and in assessing information? What does the sharing of information by means of information and communication technology have to do with moral decision making? In this chapter I will show how moral decision-making is influenced by technology and how technology is embedded in the normative structure of military practice. So-called 'neutral' technologies may cause conflicts between the various moral standards, rules and principles – referred to as 'structure' in this chapter – that characterise military practice.

2 Moral Decision-making on the Battlefield: The Philosophical Background

How can we learn to understand the role of technology in moral decision-making in modern military missions? Let's take another look at the Sangin incident. A number of problems are mentioned that at first sight appear to be logical sequences. These problems can be phrased in terms of technology (a voice link should have been in place), in terms of people (the JTAC made a wrong decision), in terms of organisation (the rules for handling confusing situations were not in place) or context (it was 'bad-guy territory' anyway). All of these approaches give insights into what went wrong in some way, however, they tend to simplify or reduce the situation to one aspect, thereby not doing justice to the complex reality in which the decision to strike was made. In order to do justice to the complexity, a more in-depth analysis is needed, which the framework of normative practice can offer. Incidentally, this focus on ethics in relation to technology is not new. Heidegger wrote about the relationship between man and technology in the early 20th century, and Jacques Ellul also discussed it. It was not until the 1990s that the philosophy of technology took an 'empirical turn', focussing on understanding technology itself and the relationship between technology and society. Contemporary philosophers of technology such as Carl Mitcham, Don Ihde, Andrew Feenberg, Peter-Paul Verbeek, Peter Kroes and Anthonie Meijers have contributed significantly to our understanding of technology and its meaning for people and society. Some of these authors acknowledge the fact that technology does not normally function in a vacuum, but is embedded in a social practice, and clearly so in military practice. In this chapter I will demonstrate how technology, which is often assumed to be neutral, actually influences the social (and thus moral) practice in which it is embedded.

3 Information and Communication Technology in Military Practice

Extrapolating the moral dimension of technology to the battlefield is not entirely new. The use of nuclear technology, anti-personnel mines, non-lethal weapons and drones has been the subject of debate for some time (Altmann et al. 2013; Royakkers and Orbons 2015). Information and communication technology (ICT) on the battlefield is a distinctive form of military technology, because it has no immediate lethal or harmful capacities. However, it enables many of the other technologies, such as UAVs, artificial intelligence and big data applications. These supposedly neutral technologies play an important role in moral decision-making in military practice. In today's complex and *ad hoc* multinational operations, the ideal is to create a strongly connected military organisation which allows synchronised and thus improved decision-making. (Alberts et al. 2002; Alberts and Hayes 2006; Alberts 2007; Smith 2006; Lambert and Scholz 2005; Soeters 2017). For example, it is possible to have immediate air support from UAVs in the event that a patrol unexpectedly comes under fire, as in the Sangin incident. Information about a patrol under attack is nowadays available at all levels of command, vertically from a unit's own line of command and horizontally from other units. This is an essential difference from traditional hierarchically structured information flows and

ETHICS AND TECHNOLOGY

coordination. However, the Sangin incident shows that it is not necessarily true that real-time information sharing makes for better military effects.

4 Moral Decision-making in Military Practice

Decisions on life or death, with which every soldier may be confronted, are inevitably moral decisions. In the Sangin incident there was little doubt that, once the pilot would push the buttons to engage, people were going to be killed. The decision in the Sangin incident was taken in a stressful and complex situation. Part of the stress was caused by uncertainty with regard to the facts (what is the direction of the firing?) and partly by uncertainty about the standards that hold for the killing of combatants (is it justified to use lethal force at a certain moment?). Moral decisions relate to the standards inherent in practice; they concern what one *should* do. There are a great many views on moral decision-making, but the following quote from Casebeer and Churchland provides an appropriate framework for our analysis:

> As moral philosophers would put it, moral reasoning is probably a species of practical reasoning about what we should do or think now, such as whether to negotiate with terrorists, not necessarily about what others have done nor about strictly empirical matters, such as whether there is water on Mars. (...) Broadly speaking, then, moral reasoning deals with cognitive acts and judgements associated with norms, or with facts as they relate to norms.
>
> 2003, pp. 170–171

An important element of this quote is the notion of 'norms'. For the purpose of this chapter, I use the concept of norms as described in the normative practice model developed by Jochemsen and Hoogland (1997). As mentioned in Chapter 1, a range of norms apply to everyday life, such as economic norms, functional norms and social norms, which can be identified explicitly in the normative practice approach. The norms for moral decision-making in military operations are partly derived from the (sub)practices in which professionals do their jobs. A sub-practice is, for example, the military pilot practice, the JTAC practice and the military medic practice. Military practice is the overarching practice with general rules and norms that hold for any military practitioner. Additionally, there are specific rules that hold for military sub-practices on top of the general norms and rules for military practice. Moral decision-making in these practices may relate to whether or not to attack persons or objects, or to assigning a certain threat level to a person or an event during a mission. These are all cognitive acts that relate to a moral norm in the practice of, for example, pilots or JTACS. Other rules and norms also often play a role in moral decision-making. There are, for instance, juridical rules and norms (is it in line with the (international) rules for armed conflict?), or economic norms (are the costs associated with this decision proportionate to the budget?). Moral decision-making is a cognitive act or judgment in which norms play a role and in which the outcome of the decision has moral significance.

Casebeer and Churchland's conception of moral decision-making lends itself well to discussing the role of technology in moral decision-making in modern military missions, because military practice is a decision- and action-oriented environment. The central concept of 'cognitive action' used by the two authors is appropriate for this decision- and action-oriented environment and the concept of 'norms' is closely linked to the theory of normative practices.

5 Normative Practice Analysis

Several philosophers in the tradition of Reformational philosophy[3] have developed a theory of normative practices over the past twenty years. The idea for such a theory came from Hoogland, Jochemsen and Glas (1997) and consisted of combining MacIntyre's (1981) theory of practice with concepts from Reformational philosophy. These authors demonstrated that normativity is inherent to medical practice (Glas 2009; Hoogland and Jochemsen 2000; Jochemsen 2006), rather than an addition to a neutral pratice. The theory of normative practices was also used by Verkerk, Hoogland, Van der Stoep and De Vries (2015) to understand the practice of engineering. This chapter analyses a new field of application in the light of the theory of normative practices, namely military practice, with particular attention being paid to the role of technology. Describing military practice as normative practice is important for understanding the role of technology in moral decisions.

5.1 *From Social Practices to Normative Practices*
The concept of a social practice was revived by Alasdair MacIntyre, who lent it a specific meaning by referring to internal and external goods, and standards by which we can judge a practice for excellence. MacIntyre's definition of 'practice' is:

---

3 Reformational philosophy is a school of thought within Christian philosophy.

ETHICS AND TECHNOLOGY

> Any coherent and complex form of socially established cooperative human activity through which goods internal to that form of activity are realized in the course of trying to achieve those standards of excellence which are appropriate to, and partially definitive of, that form of activity, with the result that human powers to achieve excellence, and human conceptions of the ends and goods involved, are systematically extended.
>
> 1981, p. 187

Jochemsen, Hoogland and Glas (1997) expanded MacIntyre's version of a social practice by arguing that social practices have specific laws or law spheres of their own and that they are therefore structurally bound by specific rules, norms and principles. The normative structure of a social practice is not only the boundary of the practice, but also has a constitutive function. Some rules and norms and procedures are what makes the practice that specific practice, in the same way as the rules of the game of chess make what chess is as a game. These rules, norms and procedures are called the structural side of a practice. A practice has a directional side, too. This is the way in which people who work in the practices 'open up' the structure; in other words, how they interpret the rules and norms of the practice and in what concrete terms they lay down the norms and whether they ultimately comply with them or not. This is often inspired by a person's cultural or religious background and is related to his/her worldview and ethos. It can vary by time and place.

5.2   *Military Practice as Normative Practice: Structure and Direction*

Military practice stems from a societal need for safety and is therefore rooted in society, but in such a way that it is not fully absorbed by the civilian society. As stated in Chapter 1, in a democratic state the use of force has been delegated to the armed forces, and military practice can be said to function on behalf of the civilian society. A distinction between civilians and military personnel exists on a number of fundamental issues. Military personnel, unlike civilians, are allowed to use lethal force without this leading to criminal prosecution, and there are specific laws applicable to military personnel, such as military disciplinary law. For the further analysis of moral decision-making in military missions, this distinction is important. Working in a practice means being less free or having different freedoms than in daily life outside that practice. After all, private acts are distinguished from military acts. Some actions and decisions are appropriate within the practice, but they would be very inappropriate outside that practice ('searching someone's house' is a good example of an action in military practice that is inappropriate outside that practice). Jochemsen and Hoogland (1997) use the term 'intrinsic normativity', or 'inner nature' of a practice, by which they mean the structural conditions that precede the practice, or the ties by which the practice is naturally bound. Intrinsic normativity is not only about internal goods, as in the practical concept of MacIntyre (1981), or about what is specific to a practice, but also about the guiding principles of a practice. In the normative practice view, the intrinsic normativity of a practice concerns the structure and direction of a practice.

5.2.1 Structure

The structure of a practice is often captured in documentation, articles, manuals and procedures and relates to the formal 'aspects'[4] of the practice. They are different for different practices. The internal organisation of the engineering practice differs from a medical practice, and differs from the military practice. These differences in structure are mainly caused by differences in the primary processes that drive these practices.

A practice often has one aspect which characterises, or rather qualifies, it. Military practice is qualified by the legal aspect, meaning that the laws applying to the legal aspect guide the other aspects (and not the other way around, as would be the case, for example, if the economic rules were to guide the legal rules, by which the practice would wind up as one that 'sells' military interventions to the highest bidder). Military practices are constitutionally bound, and actions within this practice ultimately fall under the supreme authority of a state. The monopoly of (physical) force lies with the state, and this is an indispensable premise for maintaining a just society (Besselink 2008, p. 5). As the state is bound by the Constitution, it necessarily follows that the military practice can only use force within the legal framework provided by that state. Military practice is thus limited, as well as qualified, by the legal aspect. The actions of a soldier are primarily framed by the legal standards and procedures provided by the state. They form the 'constitutive patterns of behaviour', i.e. the characteristic actions that shape military practice, but also make that practice possible. These are usually actions that relate to preventing or stopping (gross) violations of law and justice.

In the Sangin incident, pilots, data analysts, ground soldiers and a tactical air traffic controller operated in the military practice, which, as stated above, is qualified by the juridical aspect. However, each of them was also part of a distinct sub-practice. Some general rules and norms hold for each of the

---

4 By 'aspects' I am loosely referring to the aspects of reality as formulated by the Dutch philosopher Herman Dooyeweerd (1935), namely: the numerical, spatial, kinetic, physical, biotic, psychological, analytical, historical, linguistic, social, economic, aesthetic, legal, ethical, and pistic aspects.

sub-practices in military practice, for example, the rules for wearing uniforms when on duty, or the norm to have a buddy or a second-in-command. However, within the military sub-practices, different additional norms and rules exist. For example, there may be differences in 'rules of engagement', depending on the mission one is involved in. Different norms exist for pilots, JTACS and commanders regarding the checks and procedures for an airstrike.

5.2.2   Direction

In addition to the structural side of practices, the normative practice model also has a directional side of practices. 'Direction' refers to a person's life orientation; it has to do with different basic convictions about good and evil, humanity and the world, which deeply motivate practitioners to adequately perform their tasks in that practice. In military practice, this is reflected in the different ways in which force is applied. For example, there is a difference between using means of force to 'win a war' and using them to 'bring stability' to a specific region. A soldier may, for example, be most deeply driven by a world view in which social order and harmony are paramount, as in societies that have their roots in Confucianism. This motivation is very different from that of, for example, Japanese kamikaze pilots, for whom dying for their leader represented the highest honour, or from that of IS warriors who use martyrdom as a means to attain higher ideals and to reach their promised paradise.

6   Technology Connects Practices

In the previous sections, we have thematised the context in which the Sangin incident took place as a normative practice with a structural and a directional side. As noted before, describing military practice as a normative practice is crucial for understanding the role of technology in moral decisions, because technology is often important but at the same time remarkably underestimated in decision-making in military practice. Dekker (2005), for example, calls actors in modern military missions 'nodes in a network'. This terminology reveals a mechanistic view of the way military personnel operate in military operations. Developers and users of technologies often assume that the technologies themselves are neutral. They also assume that 'connecting the various nodes', i.e. connecting military and civil partners by means of technology, is a neutral activity.[5] However, various philosophers of technology have argued

---

5   See Boshuijzen-Van Burken (2016) for a discussion of the non-neutrality of military technology.

that technology is not so neutral after all, for example because technology provokes certain moral acts (Verbeek 2008), or because algorithms are not value-neutral (Kraemer et al. 2011).

The Sangin incident described at the beginning of this chapter makes clear that once technology is introduced, it is not merely a matter of 'nodes in a network' being connected. Instead, it is a matter of practices (such as the pilot practice, JTAC practice, DGS-in, commander practice, etc.) being linked by means of technology. The DGS system, which transmits video feeds to the ground units and is intended to support the JTAC, connects the pilot with the ground commander. In the Sangin incident, this connection 'muddied the waters' between the structures of the two separate practices. Inherent to the JTAC's structure is that he follows intensive and regularly recurring training in the field of interpretation of maps, aerial photographs and methods of communication. The JTAC's rules and standards are related, *inter alia*, to conducting attacks in such a way that minimal damage is inflicted on infrastructure, allies or local civilians. A JTAC is therefore focused on details of situations on the ground. The commander operates in a different sub-practice and has been trained to keep in mind the general objectives of the mission and the rules for the deployment of weapons. The commander's rules and norms therefore differ from the JTAC's and focus on the larger operational picture within which an attack is carried out. The commander's rules and norms are less concerned with detail, whereas the JTAC's rules and norms focus more on detail, such as the guidelines for distances and impact radius with regard to the use of lethal assets. Moreover, the DGS structure differs from the commander structure and from the JTAC structure. The DGS personnel's process is focused on the analysis and transmission of video images to strengthen ground commanders' and combat units' information position. The DGS's structure is therefore focused on the reliability, validity and confidentiality of information and there are rules and norms for deciding which information merits attention and which information can be left out of the picture. Within the JTAC's and the commander's structure it is not possible to acquire and evaluate information on that scale; they have not been trained in that form of information processing, but do have rules and norms on what action to take when certain information is provided.

In the Sangin incident the practices discussed above seemed to have become obscured, so that it was no longer clear which actions belonged to which practice. Procedures prescribing what should be done in the case of doubt about events were in place, but no one decided to start such a procedure after the leader at DGS-IN had raised questions on the issue via the whisper chat. There was no clear integrated structure or guideline for communication between the personnel controlling the Predator and the ground commander. Otto argues

ETHICS AND TECHNOLOGY

that technical and procedural rules must be followed, and some of these rules require the installation of additional hardware to enable two-way communication (Otto in Laster & Iannotta 2012). He refers to the technical and procedural rules, rules of engagement and authority structures that all need to be attuned to one another when (new) technology is used. These rules and regulations may not be overlooked when analysing the moral decision-making of a single person or team on the battlefield. On top of that, technology also structures and restructures (social) relationships, organisations, friendships, etcetera. A case in point is the way in which Facebook obfuscates and reinterprets the concept of 'friend', and the way it enables new forms of communication but also pre-shapes them. In the Sangin incident, many social and organisational structures were connected via ICT, such as the DGS-IN, JTAC and Predator crew. Technology influences the way in which these social structures are ordered and the way in which individuals in these structures respond to morally significant situations. In the Sangin incident, part of the communication necessarily took place through written text messages because this was dictated by technology, but not everyone had access to this mode of communication, so that the technology partly determined the lines of communication. As the situation evolved, qualified or unambiguous real-time communication through text messages became difficult, and this affected both the person writing the messages (how do you make clear that the question about the direction of the muzzle flashes is an important one?) and the reader who had to wait for the messages and interpret them while the situation called for quick action.

It appears that the obscuring of practices led to a number of concrete problems, such as misinterpretation of information and the procedural errors that followed it. As stated in other chapters of this book, moral decision-making cannot be understood without an understanding of the specific social context in which a decision is taken. The normative practice model enables us to see a soldier not only as a 'node in the network', a task performance (e.g. pressing a button) directed by rules, or a purely goal-oriented actor, but also as a person with beliefs about who he or she wants to be or how a task should be carried out correctly. These beliefs relate to the 'rules of the game' within the various practices. A pilot who does a good job does this in a different way than an engineer in the field. In contemporary military missions, practices, all of which have their own set of rules and standards, can be interconnected, which may lead to these practices becoming blurred, with potentially tragic consequences like those described above. The normative practice analysis of this friendly-fire case example shows that several partners were involved and that they were geographically dispersed. The crew in California, a DGS in Indiana and a JTAC in Afghanistan all had different roles, tasks and responsibilities. Conceptualising the work of these different partners as normative practices, which is a specific (but not the only) form of social organisation, brings to light a number of questions that are relevant to moral decision-making. For example: who is authorised to see which information and who is not, who has authority to abort a planned strike and on what grounds? The Predator crew, the DGS and the JTAC were bound in their actions by procedures, standards and rules. The Sangin case example makes clear that there are technical and procedural rules (structure) that must be followed in terms of communication. Apart from rules and regulations, the service members also had a broader vision (direction) and a certain 'drive' to carry out their tasks, as the phrase 'furiously scanned for targets' reveals. This says something about the service members' ethos. In addition, Otto's comment: 'There's women and children' (Laster and Iannotta 2012) reveals a world view in which women and children are seen in a different way than men or warriors. This influences moral decision-making, as has been discussed in the other chapters of this book.

7　Technology Itself Is Not Neutral

In the previous section I have demonstrated how technology can obscure normative practices and thus influence moral decision-making. This way of looking at things demonstrates that military decision-making does not take place in a vacuum, but rather in a very unique social structure. In addition to the notion that technology influences social structures, I will show in the section below that technology itself is not neutral but can be morally charged.

The technologies that played a role in the Sangin incident included the aircraft itself (the Predator) and IT systems that connected the control stations in California and Indiana with each other. These include radios, satellites, screens, chat interfaces, the Internet, geographical information systems (GIS), maps, buttons and sticks for controlling the aircraft, missiles, etc. These technologies played a role in the moral decision to launch the strike. For example, the DGS-IN saw information on their screen (i.e. the direction of the muzzle flashes) on the basis of which a moral judgment was made: the judgment about who was an enemy who had to be killed. The technology also made it possible to share (moral) concerns, namely by typing these concerns in the chat box. The chat box had a built-in 'moral' option, i.e. the option for whisper chats, which allowed potentially important information to be held back. Holding back information is a choice with consequences for moral decision-making, because the information withheld may influence the decision whether or not to fire. The option of whether or not to share information with everyone was deliberately built into the design of the DGS interface (perhaps to avoid information overload), but this came at the expense of transparency and the possibility to express concerns. Technology is thus not neutral, as the design of technology implicitly (or sometimes explicitly) expresses a certain value, for example transparency. Another example of the non-neutrality of technology is the use of heat cameras, as a result of which surfaces that are larger or warmer (thus giving a deeper thermal image) appear to be more important than surfaces that give off less heat or are smaller. The pitfall here is that attention then automatically shifts to the surface that gives a deeper thermal image, for example a car with a warm engine, and not to the child standing next to the car, or, as in the Sangin example, to muzzle flashes instead of to the people on the spot. Another non-neutral aspect of technology is the fact that it often works according to the logic of reduction and amplification. In the case of the Sangin incident, the thermal images did show the temperature of surfaces (i.e. temperature was amplified), but colours, precise forms and emotions were concealed. In this way, both friend and foe were reduced to a spot on a screen. Finally, there is the non-neutrality of the algorithms that enable the projection of thermal images on a screen. It is a choice of designers and sometimes users of thermal images to set a threshold value and this threshold value determines which temperatures become visible in what way, for example in which colour or intensity. The choice can be made to set a high threshold value, so that only very hot surfaces emit a thermal image, such as weapons being fired or vehicles with engines running, or to set a low threshold value, so that, for example, people and animals with a lower temperature render an accurate thermal image on the screen. All these forms of non-neutrality of technology can play a role in moral decision-making.

8   Conclusion

The critical reader might observe that in military practice there has always been a great deal of cooperation between (sub)practices by means of technology. This is certainly true. However, the diverse practices within the overarching military practice were traditionally linked through hierarchical structures and means of communication. The more traditional means of communication, such as the radio, served to confirm this hierarchical structure, enabling vertical information exchange via lines of command. What is different nowadays is that all the various ways of working are connected by means of information and communication technologies. These so-called 'neutral' technologies may cause clashes between the various norms, rules and principles – referred to as 'structure' in this chapter – that characterise these different practices. It has suddenly become unclear – or less clear – which rule should prevail and who holds which role. Due to the hierarchical nature of military practice, this problem did not occur before: in the event of clashes, the solution was dictated by the hierarchy. With the introduction of information and communication technology, the number of interactions has increased and the interactions are direct and synchronous in time. As a result, there is an increased likelihood of rules and guidelines conflicting with one another. The conclusion is therefore that the technology linking ground forces, intelligence personnel and the local commander, which was assumed to be neutral, links practices that were previously unlinked. And in so far as they did interact in the past, this occurred along clear lines, namely via a commander who communicated with another commander. Looking more closely at the individual level of the different practices in which soldiers make decisions and act, we can conclude that information and communication technologies may in fact have been what caused the tragedy at the Sangin River. The assumption was that it was clear what the message was and which rule would prevail, when in reality there was no clarity at all.

In this chapter I have suggested that the theory of normative practices may shed light on the question of why the decision to fire was made, and how this decision was influenced by technology. In order to prevent further incidents, it is essential that soldiers become aware that technology not only makes for easier communication, but that it might also cause an unnoticed blurring of dividing lines between practices. It is therefore important for soldiers to identify the potential pitfalls of modern military operations, both in relation to their own day-to-day practice and in cooperation with others, in particular with regard to specific responsibilities and rules relating to the technology used.

Literature

Alberts, D.S. (2007). 'Agility, Focus, and Convergence: The Future of Command and Control.' *The International C2 Journal* 1(1), 1–30.

Alberts, D.S., Garstka, J.J., Hayes, R.E. and Signori, D.A. (2002). *Understanding Information Age Warfare.* Washington, D.C.: CCRP Publication Series.

Alberts, D.S. and Hayes, R.E. (2006). *Understanding Command and Control, The Future of Command and Control.* Washington, D.C.: CCRP Publication Series.

Altmann, J., Asaro, P., Sharkey, N. and Sparrow, R. (2013). 'Armed Military Robots: Editorial.' *Ethics and Information Technology,* 15(2), 73.

ETHICS AND TECHNOLOGY 81

Besselink, L.F.M. (2008). 'Geweldsmonopolie, Grondwet en krijgsmacht.' *Publikaties van de Staatsrechtkring, 26,* 67–124.

Boshuijzen-Van Burken, C. (2016). 'Beyond Technological Mediation: A Normative Practice Approach.' *Techné 20*(3), 177–197. DOI: https://doi.org/10.5840/techne20 1671949.

Casebeer, W.D. and Churchland, P.S. (2003). 'The Neural Mechanisms of Moral Cognition: A Multiple-Aspect Approach to Moral Judgment and Decision-Making.' *Biology and Philosophy 18*(1), 169–194.

Dekker, A. (2005). 'A Taxonomy of Network Centric Warfare Architectures.' *Proceedings of the Systems Engineering/Test and Evaluation Conference,* November 2005, Brisbane, Australia.

Dooyeweerd, H. (1935). *De Wijsbegeerte Der Wetsidee.* Vol. 1–3. Amsterdam: H.J. Paris.

Glas, G. (2009). Modellen van 'integratie' in de psychologie en psychiatrie (II) ° het normatieve praktijk model. *Psyche en geloof 20* (3/4), 165–177.

Hoogland, J. and Jochemsen, H. (2000). 'Professional Autonomy and the Normative Structure of Medical Practice.' *Theoretical Medicine and Bioethics 21*(5), 457–475.

Jochemsen, H. en Hoogland, J. (1997). 'De normatieve structuur van de medische praktijk.' In: Jochemsen, H. and Glas, G. (eds.). *Verantwoord medisch handelen. Proeve van een christelijke medische ethiek.* Vol. Lindeboomreeks, part 10 (pp. 64–99). Amsterdam: Buijten and Schipperheijn.

Jochemsen, H. (2006). 'Normative Practices and Theoretical Ethics and Morality.' *Philosophia Reformata 71*(1), 96–112.

Kraemer, F., Overveld, K. van and Peterson, M. Is There an Ethics of Algorithms? *Ethics and Information Technology 13,* no. 3 (2011): 251–260. DOI: https://doi.org/10.1007/s10676-010-9233-7.

Lambert, D.A. and Scholz, J.B. (2005). *A Dialectic for Network Centric Warfare.* Fairbairn, Australia: DSTO.

Laster, J. and Iannotta, B. (2012). 'Learning from Fratricide-US Deaths in Sangin Valley Bring Long-Sought Tactical Intel Changes.' *C4ISR-Journal of Net-Centric Warfare 11*(2), 24–27.

MacIntyre, A. (1981). *After Virtue: A Study in Moral Theory.* London: Duckworth.

Royakkers L., Orbons S. (2015). 'Design for Values in the Armed Forces: Nonlethal Weapons and MilitaryRobots.' In: J. van den Hoven, P. Vermaas and I. van de Poel (eds), *Handbook of Ethics, Values, and Technological Design* (pp 613–638). Dordrecht: Springer. DOI: https://doi.org/10.1007/978-94-007-6970-0_28

Smith, E.A. (2006). *Complexity, Networking and Effects-Based Approaches to Operations.* Washington, D.C.: CCRP Publication Series.

Soeters, J. (2017). 'Information Sharing in Military and Security Operations.' In: I. Goldenberg, J. Soeters and W.H. Dean (eds.), *Information Sharing in Military*

Operations (pp. 1–15). Cham: Springer International Publishing. DOI: https://doi.org/10.1007/978-3-319-42819-2_1.

Verbeek, P.P. Obstetric Ultrasound and the Technological Mediation of Morality: A Postphenomenological Analysis. *Human Studies 31*, no. 1 (2008): 11–26.

Verkerk, M.J., Hoogland, J., Stoep, J. and Vries, M.J. (2015). *Philosophy of Technology: An Introduction for Technology and Business Students*. Abingdon: Routledge.

CHAPTER 7

An Organisational Perspective on Military Ethics

Eric-Hans Kramer, Herman Kuipers and Miriam de Graaff

'I surrendered my moral conscience to the fact I was a soldier, and therefore a cog in a relatively low position of a great machine.' Commander of an *Einsatzgruppe*, at the Nuremberg trials
PICK 1993, p. 187

∴

1 Introduction

Discussions on military ethics often solely focus on the challenges, dilemmas and actions in military missions. Which makes sense for two reasons. First, soldiers' actions have potentially large and possibly harmful impact for all factions involved, including themselves, their colleagues and individuals and organizations that find themselves in the military organisation's environment, noted in the other contributions in this book as well. As set out in Chapter 1, soldiers are moral agents and their moral agency gives them moral responsibility to act in such a way that they are able to reflect on the ethical aspects of their profession. In the Dutch military, the Code of Conduct therefore states that in a complex situation all employees must act according to their weighted judgment regarding that particular situation, taking into account all parties' values, rights and interests that are at stake (cf. De Graaff 2018). Second, this highly demanding and complex environment inherently leads to an abundance of moral issues on an individual level, such as moral stress, moral disengagement and even moral injury (cf., Molendijk 2020; De Graaff, Giebels & Verweij 2020)

Even though this focus on the challenges, dilemmas and actions is understandable, there are many factors that are not quite as obvious but influence military practice nonetheless. When a group of soldiers is confronted with moral dilemmas, we are dealing with a specific group (which has been composed in advance), operating in a specific mission with specific goals (which have been formulated in advance), which is part of a larger organised system (which has been designed that way), with certain capabilities (in which they

© KONINKLIJKE BRILL NV, LEIDEN, 2022 | DOI:10.1163/9789004512474_008

may or may not have been sufficiently trained), with certain assets (which have been purchased and maintained), and with the support of a network of other units (which have been brought together in a mission). Verweij (2009, p. 15) notes that in applied ethics the focus is on reflection of a certain profession, with military ethics focusing on reflection on ethical issues in military practice. Military practice is shaped by the preparation, facilitation and concrete implementation of the armed forces' tasks (Verweij 2009, p. 24; cf. also Chapter 1). In other words, military practice is an organised practice, making the design of this practice an issue relevant to address.

Therefore, this chapter focuses on the question of how the design of organisations – also referred to as the structure or architecture – influences moral responsibility and the organization's interventions. We will start this chapter with a historical case that highlights the complexity of the issue of responsibility in military organisations. From this we will conclude that the military profession is characterized by a specific area of tension. We will argue that, in practice, on the one hand it is important that soldiers obey a political and bureaucratic authority, while on the other, bearing in mind the complexity of military practice, autonomous judgment and the associated freedom of action is also essential. The chapter is premised on the notion that the way in which the military practice is organised is decisive for the way in which soldiers can deal with this area of tension. On the basis of socio-technical organizational theory, we distinguish between 'the bureaucratic regime' and 'the flexible regime' (Kuipers et al. 2020). These two types of regime represent ideal-typical extremes in terms of the way practices in organisations can be designed. These extremes each have a different effect on the way soldiers are able to deal with the area of tension in question and, with that, a very different effect on moral responsibility. This chapter will make clear that the design of organisations is *preconditional* for soldiers to behave in a morally responsible manner. Organisational design can either hinder or promote ethical violations and misconduct (cf. Kaptein 2008). However, such preconditions will never have a determining effect on moral agents' moral responsibility.

2 Eichmann and the Question of Responsibility

An example in which the design of organisations in relation to responsibility takes centre-stage is Hannah Arendt's analysis of the trial of Adolf Eichmann in Jerusalem. Adolf Eichmann was an SS officer in the Second World War and played a key role in organising the Holocaust. For instance, he was the person who organised the so-called Wannsee Conference. At this conference, top-level decisions were made on how the destruction of the European Jewish population was to be organised. After the Second World War, Eichmann fled to Argentina, where he was abducted by the Israeli Mossad in 1960 and taken to Jerusalem. He was put on trial there in 1961. That trial culminated in a death sentence, which was carried out on 1 June 1962.

Arendt attended Eichmann's trial and published her analysis in a series of newspaper articles and in her book *Eichmann in Jerusalem* (2007). In her analysis, Arendt outlines a special dilemma for the judges in this trial (2007, pp. 40–41). Normally, a crime is a crime because it goes against the law. As regards the Eichmann trial, however, this was not the case. Arendt argued that in a certain sense Eichmann even behaved impeccably (2007, pp. 43–44):

> '(…) he acted in accordance with the rule, examined the order issued to him for its 'manifest' legality, namely regularity; he did not have to fall back upon his 'conscience', since he was not one of those who were unfamiliar with the laws of his country. The exact opposite was the case.' (Quotation marks in the original)

Arendt emphasised that Eichmann was an officicer in a bureaucratic apparatus that was part of a functioning state system. She even observed that Eichmann reviled ss colleagues who tried to shirk the dirty work. Even when faced with surviving relatives of his victims, Eichmann appeared unable to suppress a certain professional pride.

Following Eichmann's trial, Arendt introduced the idea of 'the banality of evil'. According to this idea, behind the face of this man was not a manifest monster, but a bureaucratised officer who concentrated on carrying out rules. The idea of the banality of evil expresses the notion that extremely unethical behaviour need not primarily be a consequence of individual evil, but of the thoughtlessness of a collective of obedient officials who have surrendered their authentic thinking faculties – and with that their responsibility – to a bureaucratic system and, as a result, are blind to the outcomes that system produces. To Arendt, this conclusion was much more disturbing than the possibility that Eichmann was an evidently evil individual. The Eichmann case demonstrates the profound personality-deforming effects a bureaucratic regime can have and to what catastrophes it can lead. If banality can lead to genocide, perhaps we must fear that the Holocaust was not just an exceptional event. In fact, as Arendt points out, it may well have been caused by the characteristics of an important institutional form in our modern society: bureaucracy.

The philosopher Zygmunt Bauman (1989) argues that the Holocaust would have been inconceivable without an underlying bureaucratic apparatus. He argues that (a) instrumental bureaucratic rationality is incapable of preventing the Holocaust and (b) it was specifically in an instrumental culture of bureaucracy that an idea such as the Holocaust could ultimately evolve and be implemented. Instrumental rationality refers to a an exclusively rule based way of processing information (i.e. by instruments) without taking account of the content of the information itself. In a strictly instrumental sense, there is no distinction between developing and implementing procedures to assemble a car, to regulate the management of public gardens or to organise the deportation of a substantial part of the European Jewish population towards the gas chambers. For that reason, instrumental logic can (deliberately) be used to pursue immoral objectives, and the context of a constitutional state governed by the rule of law even provides for a degree of justification for this. It is not without reason that bureaucracies are sometimes called systems of organised irresponsibility (Beck 1995, p. 63).

3 Discussions on Moral Responsibility and Bureaucracy

Arendt's discussion of the Eichmann case has given rise to much debate, with the issue of responsibility and bureaucratisation being central themes. The Jewish community blamed her for lending a certain justification to Eichmann's actions with the idea of 'the banality of evil'. This is because it makes him appear a victim of circumstances: a somewhat simple civil servant who had surrendered his faculties for authentic thinking to an extensive and complex system that compelled rule-following behaviour. Historical research by Stangneth (2014) has shown that Eichmann was in fact a fanatical adherent to the Nazi ideology. De Swaan also argues that the idea of banality is in fact not at all applicable to the figure of Eichmann. You might even say that a top official in the Nazi hierarchy like Eichmann used bureaucratic organisational techniques to his advantage, rather than that he was a victim of them. De Swaan states the following on the subject (2014, p. 29):

> Arendt's thesis on the 'banality of evil' does not stand critical scrutiny, certainly not as applied to Adolf Eichmann or other Nazi-leaders, nor for that matter to rank-and-file killers. Her model might, however, fit the countless minor middlemen of the Holocaust: the administrators in the civil registry who passed on the names of the prospective victims, the local police who rounded them up, the engineers who transported them in cattle cars, the contractors who built the gas chambers and supplied the extermination camps ... most of them were in a sense banal.

Indeed, Arendt seems to have underestimated Eichmann's ideological motivation. De Swaan also criticizes Bauman. By focusing on the disturbing aspects of instrumental bureaucracy, Bauman ignores the barbaric and regressive aspects of genocide (De Swaan 2015, p. 44). De Swaan argues an intermediate position: situational and therefore organisational factors have a major influence on the behaviour of individuals (De Swaan's central concept is 'compartmentalisation'), but the behaviour of individuals cannot be fully explained or justified by this. All kinds of individual factors are involved, but also, for example, macro-sociological factors (culture and history of a particular society and of groups within it). Although De Swaan thus accuses Arendt and Bauman of overstating their argument, he too believes that the design of organisations influences ethical behaviour and is therefore relevant in moral functioning.

The above analyses show that the concept of moral responsibility is a complex one. Ethical violations need not only be the result of violating rules, but also of blindly following them. In addition, it appears that moral responsibility is not only a purely individual issue, but also has to do with the organised context in which moral agents operate. However, there is still confusion about the mechanism by which the design of organisations influences moral responsibility. While reference is made to instrumental rationality, 'cogs in an extensive machinery' and compartmentalisation, the mechanism at work needs to be explored in more detail. It is precisely in this respect that organizational theory can make a contribution, as we will see below.

4 Moral Responsibility and the Area of Tension in the Military Profession

The military organisation is a special organisation because the question of responsibility is inevitably linked to its fundamental character as an organisation charged with carrying out the tasks arising from the state's monopoly of force (cf. also Chapter 1). The military organisation applies force in an instrumental way, i.e. in the service of objectives it has not formulated itself and within a framework of rules and procedures. The difference between 'legitimate' force and other forms of force determines the identity of the military organisation. According to the constitutional definition, soldiers in democratic societies are the instrumental implementers of the objectives set by the political leadership. That is essential, because in a democratic society we do not want the military organisation to use force as it sees fit. It is this idea of 'legitimate force' that constitutes the formal basis for the morality of military practice.

Huntington (1957) emphasises that for that reason 'moral responsibility' in military practice means obedience towards bureaucratic authority. However, Huntington at the same time emphasises that there are limits to responsibility in the sense of blind obedience. Where blind obedience could lead to catastrophes as a result of circumstances that are unknown, responsibility may also mean that soldiers should ignore their instructions. On the one hand, therefore, we want soldiers who use force within the parameters set for legitimate force. On the other hand, we assume military practice to be so complex that a one-dimensional *Befehl ist Befehl* is undesirable. This area of tension is inherent to the military profession.

Moral responsibility in practice takes shape by soldiers bringing their obedience to bureaucratic authority in line with local circumstances. They do this by making use of their judgment and freedom of action and by observing more general principles such as those expressed in humanitarian law. This modus operandi is discussed by Lipsky (1980), among others. He argues that the work of officials at the lowest level in government organisations (teachers, police officers, public health workers, etc.) is often difficult to prescribe exactly on the basis of rules and is difficult to monitor precisely. As a result, 'street-level bureaucrats' possess what Lipsky refers to as 'discretion', i.e. a certain natural autonomy, which gives them an important role in how policy is shaped (1980, p. 16). In this context, it is up to street-level bureaucrats to solve unique problems that have a complex relationship with the applicable rules.

The question is, however, how the organisation of military practice influences the way in which military personnel can deal with the area of tension that lies at the heart of their profession. The answer to this question is further elaborated upon below. We will juxtapose two ideal-typical organisation designs with each other. The 'bureaucratic regime' focuses mainly on organising blind obedience, while the 'flexible regime' tries to create the preconditions for latitude and freedom of action. In view of the complexity of military practice, we assume that blind obedience is undesirable and that, for this reason, there must always be latitude for independent judgment and the corresponding freedom of action. However, this does not mean that as long as people are given enough latitude, moral responsibility will follow automatically. Not only does "organisation" merely play a preconditional role, albeit an essential one, also setting up latitude at the operational level creates specific pitfalls that are of elementary relevance in the context of moral responsibility.

5   The Bureaucratic Regime and Responsibility

The idea that organisations should enforce strictly rule-following behaviour has long been dominant in organisational sciences. This idea is still an important inspiration behind developments in some new (technological) business systems (cf. Chapter 6). According to socio-technical business theory, a 'bureaucratic regime' is characterised by a focus on perfecting internal processes (Kuipers et al. 2020). A bureaucratic regime presupposes a stable and predictable environment. This forms the basis for aspiring to strictly rule-driven internal processes.

The need for bureaucratisation originally stems from an increasingly complex social and societal system and a state apparatus that wishes to control it: taxes must be levied, who owns which plot of land must be recorded, et cetera (Beniger 1986). According to the sociologist Max Weber, there is a crucial difference between bureaucracy as it was in traditional societies and as it is in modern times. This difference is caused by rationalisation. Whereas in a traditional bureaucracy authority was exercised along clientelist lines (cronyism), modern times are characterised by attempts to base bureaucratic authority on rules. According to Weber's description, the rational bureaucracy is characterised by the following points (see Kuipers et al. 2020, p. 151):

- all tasks are necessarily carried out according to a consistent system of abstract rules;
- positions or roles are divided into highly specialised tasks in order to achieve the organisational objectives;
- tasks are organised in a hierarchical structure, in which the authority of superiors over subordinates is defined;
- superiors adopt an impersonal attitude in dealing with each other and with subordinates;
- appointments in a bureaucracy must be based on qualifications, and promotion decisions on the basis of merit.

In this way, a rational bureaucracy realises the ideal of instrumental logic through maximum division of labour. Splitting tasks into a maximum number of smaller sub-steps results in a fragmented whole of narrow tasks. This forms the basis for designing a 'consistent system of abstract rules' to perform the tasks. The idea of instrumental bureaucracy has been further developed in organisational studies in Frederick Taylor's concept of scientific management. He looked mainly at production organisations to find 'the one best way of organizing' based on – then current – ideas about scientific analysis of tasks.

This leads to organisations in which thinking and acting are largely separated (Kuipers et al. 2020). Ultimately, scientific management strives to bring about an organisation that functions as a machine (Morgan 2006), or as Pick puts it (1993, p. 175): 'the machine is elevated to the sublime'. Moral responsibility in such organisations means showing willingness to adapt to the proposed 'one best way of organising' (Verkerk 2004, p. 77).

Ideas about designing organisations as machines shaped thinking in the military organisation years before they were applied and perfected in the public sector by means of 'scientific management'. In fact, developments of this kind are inspired by the organisation of military forces. Morgan (2006) shows that Frederick the Great was led by 'the machine metaphor' when organising the Prussian army, while Toulmin (2001) points to a similar trend in Maurice of Orange's army. According to Bousquet (2009), this type of development in the organisation of armies fitted in with the broader scientific world view emerging from the seventeenth century onwards.

Organisational structure is a connecting and therefore integrating factor in organisations with regard to the many factors that shape practice in the background (Kuipers 1989; De Sitter 2000). Organising entails dividing related activities into sub-activities and connecting them again through a structure. An organisational structure can be thought of as a skeleton, and human behaviour and interaction as the tissue attached to the skeleton (Bate et al. 2000). The skeleton's design defines the identity of the 'cog' as well as the complexity of the network in which it functions. In terms of task design (Hackman et al. 1975): the more split up a task is, the less identity it has, i.e. the less it will appear a meaningful part of a whole. In complex military operations, for example, groups and individuals may entirely lose sight of how their actions contribute to the completion of the mission.

Not only does the structural design influence the degree of structural complexity, but also the composition of groups, the manner in which the work is supported by (technical) systems and the part of the environment personnel come into contact with, as well as the means and possibilities at their disposal to deal with problems. A division of tasks resulting in a group of soldiers having to operate in isolation in an unsafe area, while at the same time being crucially dependent on support that they cannot influence ('isolated dependence', see Trist et al. 1963), will increase the chance of anxiety and stress reactions. The excesses of violence in the Vietnamese village of My Lai show the consequences these emotional states can have, as described in Chapter 4.

6 The Bureaucratic Regime in Unpredictable Conditions

The pursuit of a rational bureaucracy that functions on the basis of rules and tries to banish inequality is a major foundation of our society. However, any system that tries to subject all behaviour to detailed rules on the basis of these principles will run into difficulties in unpredictable circumstances. One might even wonder whether conditions of perfect stability exist at all, or whether they are a purely theoretical possibility (De Sitter 2000). As labour is increasingly divided into executive activities, a more complex structure of regulatory activities needs to be set up in order to coordinate and supervise the whole. Also this regulatory structure can in turn be split into sub-tasks. A complex structure of regulatory tasks ultimately leads to a steep control pyramid, which ultimately leads to a complex structure with simple tasks (Kuipers et al. 2020). Such a structure increases an organisation's dependence on stable conditions.

Military history shows that 'machine-like' organisations have difficulties dealing with complex and changing conditions. In this context, Van Creveld (1985) discusses examples of the British Army in the First World War and the US army in the Vietnam War. Van Creveld's discussion of the British army during the First World War is mainly about military effectiveness. Notorious in this respect is the enormous bloodshed during trench warfare in the First World War, when troops were ordered to march towards enemy machine-gun fire in a tightly organised manner. Equally notorious is the example of infantry troops being shelled by artillery units while keeping to an elaborately detailed plan of attack, even though conditions at the front had changed in the meantime (Van Creveld 1985, p. 160). The top brass of the organisation were sometimes completely unaware of the actual conditions soldiers were facing.

Military history also offers plenty of examples of how a bureaucratic regime can lead to irresponsible behaviour. Gabriel and Savage (1979) talk about the use of the 'body count' as a measure of the objective performance of units in the Vietnam War, which could lead to civilian casualties being included in the performance index, and possibly even deliberately being made. Furthermore, bureaucracy mainly arouses extrinsic motivation in people (status, money, power), as opposed to intrinsic motivation (striving for high-quality and valuable work) (see Kuipers et al. 2020). This can cause people to try to earn impressive decorations for unimpressive behaviour. Gabriel and Savage's best-known example is the officer who earned a Purple Heart ('Wounded in Action') for injuries sustained during a grenade attack while visiting a brothel (1979, p. 15). If this kind of behaviour becomes widespread, it will erode public trust in the organisation and among people. It can lead to a 'betrayal of what's right' (Shay 1994), meaning that people feel betrayed by (people within) the organisation (cf. also Chapter 5). Similarly, Gabriel and Savage (1979) show that the far-reaching bureaucratisation of the US Army ultimately proved to fundamentally undermine the morality of the officers' corps.

Bureaucratic regimes mobilise all types of negative professional behaviour ('rat behaviour') such as hiding behind formal responsibility, careerism, all sorts of hatred and malice among people (Kuipers et al. 2020) and even sadism (Fromm 1973). Shifting responsibility to an extensive bureaucratic system, is a specific form of 'moral disengagement', (see Bandura 1986); cf. also Chapter 3). Although bureaucracy is intended as an archetype of exemplary rationality, what is described above could hardly be farther removed from the idea of the detached and rational bureaucrat who makes pure judgments.

7 The Flexible Regime and Responsibility

If we assume that conditions of complete predictability and stability do not exist, this has consequences for the organisation of moral responsibility. The fact that a military organisation cannot be a system entirely programmed by rules is the very reason it pays attention to ethics. A military organisation operates in conditions that are uncertain, changeable and dynamic and where various parties in its environment react intelligently. These are referred to as conditions of dynamic complexity (Kramer 2007). These circumstances require operators at various levels to use their judgment to assess the circumstances ('sensemaking') and to choose a course of action on that basis. In that sense, sense making is in essence inherently associated with operators who are most closely involved in operations. In dynamically complex conditions, a unit may be forced to act before it has been able to gain a full understanding of the circumstances. This idea is at the heart of Karl Weick's so-called 'enactment theory' (Weick 1979) and 'enactment' plays an important role in the practice of military organisations (Isenberg 1985; Kramer 2007; Moorkamp 2019). After an action, enactment can result in operators coming to realise that it involved ethically problematic aspects. This theoretical idea can be observed in the narratives that were reported by De Graaff (2018).

This has consequences for organising moral responsibility. An organisation that operates in circumstances of dynamic complexity must offer moral agents the latitude to act morally responsibly, just as this latitude is important in regard to other functional job requirements. This presupposes that, although a unit may strive for achieving certain standards (e.g. based on humanitarian law), it must assess in concrete situations what these standards specifically mean and how they relate to other (moral/ethical) standards. This presupposes that the agents fighting at the front of operations have the ability to act as ethically as possible under the circumstances. 'As ethically as possible' because ethics is a job requirement that may constantly clash with other job requirements at the front of operations. Of crucial importance, therefore, is the question of the extent to which military unit in which moral agents are active upholds ethical standard, gives moral agents latitude to act in ethical responsible ways, and offers them room to reflect on the way these standards have been put in practice.

If a flexible regime perceives moral responsibility in this way, what does a flexible regime look like in terms of design principles? Instead of the bureaucratic regime's principle of maximum division of labour, the principle of minimum division of labour is applied. Division of labour is a defining feature of organisations, but flexible regimes attempt to limit this as much as possible. One way to achieve this is through functional deconcentration. This means that groups and units are not formed on the basis of specialism. Functional deconcentration means that all the necessary specialisms for the performance of an entire task are brought together in a group. This will ensure that a group has comprehensive insight into a task and not just insight into one specialized aspect. This comprehensive insight is a precondition for the judgment and freedom of action of moral agents. Based on this principle, an organisation is built consisting of complex tasks and simple structures. A trend in this direction was in evidence, for example, in the Netherlands armed forces during missions in Bosnia, where combined infantry and cavalry units were given overall responsibility over a section of an area (Kramer 2007), or in Uruzgan in Afghanistan, where patrols at the lowest level were carried out with combined units (Kramer, De Waard, De Graaf 2012). These were temporary task forces, assembled on a much more *ad hoc* basis compared to larger regular units that are often structured on the basis of specialism (land, air, and sea forces, specific arms and branches, further specialised support, etc.). Military history provides several examples of armies that successfully attempted to organise room for manoeuvre at the executive level (Van Creveld 1985, p. 270):

> The fact that, historically speaking, those armies have been most successful which did not turn their troops into automatons, did not attempt to control everything from the top, and allowed subordinate commanders considerable latitude has been abundantly demonstrated.

These ideas about flexibility were developed mainly from the perspective of military effectiveness and not from the perspective of moral responsibility. The most discussed example is that of the German Wehrmacht in the Second

World War, which used a system of *Auftragstaktik* (Visser and Brouwer 2007). This system is based on the idea that lower units should not simply apply rules, but must be given autonomy to determine independently how a certain goal can be achieved (assignments specify *what* must be achieved, not *how* it should be achieved). *Auftragstaktik* is portrayed by Van Creveld as a philosophy that permeated all aspects of the functioning of the organisation: its leadership and the composition of its units, but also, for example, recruitment. On the design of that type of armies, Van Creveld (1985, p. 269) argues:

> The more numerous and differentiated the departments into which an organization is divided, the larger the number of command echelons superimposed upon each other; the higher decision thresholds, and the more specialized its individual members, then the greater the amount of information processing that has to go on inside an organisation.

Van Creveld underlines here the problem of decreasing information-processing capabilities arising from structural complexity, which in turn arises from an increasing division of labour. For this reason, he argues in favour of self-contained units at a low hierarchical level.

These examples show that the conditions for room for regulatory capacity at the executive level are created by means of the architecture of the organisation. In this respect, the design of organisations has a major impact on moral responsibility. The power of judgment, and latitude to act on the basis of this judgment, are essential preconditions for morally responsible behaviour, and it is the architecture of the organisation that creates the conditions for this. It is impossible beforehand to determine in a general sense how this should be worked out in a specific organisation for a specific operation (for example: exactly how much room for manoeuvre is desirable?). However, the principles based on which organisations are designed in this case are significantly different from those in a bureaucratic regime.

8 Moral Responsibility in an Intractable Practice

In this chapter, we started the discussion regarding the influence of organisational design on military personnel's ethical functioning, by addressing the tension inherently connected to the military profession. That is, the issue of obedience to a bureaucratic authority on the one hand and the need for autonomous judgment and associated room for manoeuvre on the other. However, it is clear that this area of tension gives rise to various difficulties in practice, both for the bureaucratic regime and for the flexible regime.

On the one hand, situations may arise in which a bureaucratic authority attempts to enforce blind obedience, while the objective being pursued thereby is highly at odds with the real conditions in which the organisation finds itself. The more the design of the organisation and regulations are at odds with the demands arising from the problem context, the higher the likelihood that moral agents will experience conflicts. In military contexts this pattern can be discerned in the stories of traumatised soldiers. Lifton (1973) analysed the stories of Vietnam veterans and discusses the typical example of soldiers who – after force had been used – turned to 'moral authorities' (senior officers, chaplains and psychologists) for help with their conflicts of conscience. Attempts by these authorities in particular to convince them that they were war heroes turned out extremely traumatic for them. It led them to believe that they were part of an immoral political-military system. According to Lifton, this experience of a 'counterfeit universe' (a universe of moral deception) plays a central role in psychological trauma among veterans. Recent research confirms that moral conflicts are an important factor in the development of psychological trauma in veterans. Nowadays the concept of 'moral injury' is used in this context (Shay 1994; Litz et al. 2008; Molendijk 2020; cf. also Chapter 5).

On the other hand, it is not self-evident that this area of tension could be eliminated by application of a flexible regime. Although such a regime aims to create the latitude required for moral responsibility, this does not mean that this latitude automatically leads to ethically responsible behaviour. Quite frequently, the opposite is the case. In organisations in which people are convinced of certain questionable ideas, judgment and autonomy may in fact be used to pursue these questionable ideas even more energetically. There are countless examples from military history in which military units committed all kinds of misconduct that were possible precisely because of the room for manoeuvre available to these units. A related example that indicates that autonomy can have adverse effects is the abuses committed in Abu Ghraib prison in Iraq in 2003. Here prisoners were mistreated and tortured by a group of American service members (cf. Chapters 2 and 4). Although Abu Ghraib certainly is not an example of a deliberately designed flexible organization, it does indicate that setting up the organizational preconditions for autonomy and judgement is certainly different from adopting a laissez faire attitude. Zimbardo (2007) attributes this behaviour to, among other things, to the fact that these soldiers were working in extremely dangerous and unhygienic conditions, where contradictory ethical guidelines for behaviour applied. For example, prison guards were asked by the secret service to break prisoners psychologically prior to their interrogation, and higher command showed no interest whatsoever in what was happening inside the prison (Hersh 2004).

9 Conclusions

Military personnel who are confronted with morally critical situations in practice need to have moral judgment and freedom of action in order to deal with these situations adequately. At the same time, in an instrument of force such as the military, it is essential that force is applied legitimately, i.e. in line with the objectives and frameworks set by the higher (political) authorities. As was discussed above, according to Huntington (1957), responsibility may also mean that soldiers should ignore instructions. In this chapter, we have tried to demonstrate that moral responsibility does not come about by individual powers of reflection alone. Given that the military practice is an organised practice, the design of the military organisation has a significant impact on this process. An organisation divides tasks, thereby influencing the section of the environment on which military personnel are focused, and determines the composition of groups. It also influences the nature of the dependencies on other subsystems and provides groups with (technical) resources. In this chapter, we have juxtaposed two ways of designing organisations and looked at how they influence moral responsibility. We have seen how the ideal-typical bureaucratic regime wishing to enforce blind obedience may run into difficulties because this may clash with the complexity of the practice. By contrast, the ideal-typical flexible regime tries to incorporate latitude and freedom of action and may run into difficulties because non-centralised room for manoeuvre can lead to all kinds of undesirable behaviour, both at individual and group level. It seems clear that granting responsibility must go hand in hand with setting clear ethical guidelines and that everyone in a military unit must be thoroughly aware of the importance of certain moral and ethical standards. One could say that there should be an *esprit de corps* that provides a foundation for ethical conduct in practice.

Literature

Arendt, H. (2007). *Eichmann in Jeruzalem. De banaliteit van het kwaad.* Amsterdam: Olympus. Original title: *Eichmann in Jerusalem. A Report on the Banality of Evil* (1963).

Bate, P., Khan, R., Pye, A. (2000). 'Towards a Culturally Sensitive Approach to Organization Structuring: Where Organization Design Meets Organization Development.' *Organization Science*, 11(2): 197–211.

Bandura, A. (1986). *Social Foundations of Thought and Action: A Social Cognitive Theory*. Upper Saddle River, NJ: Prentice-Hall, Inc.

Bauman, Z. (1989). *Modernity and the Holocaust*. London: Polity Press.

Beck, U. (1995). *Ecological Politics in an Age of Risk*. Cambridge: Polity Press.

Beniger, J.R. (1986). *The Control Revolution. Technological and Economic Origins of the Information Society*. Cambridge, MA: Harvard University Press.

Bousquet, A. (2009). *The Scientific Way of Warfare. Order and Chaos on the Battlefields of Modernity*. London: Hurst Publishers.

Creveld, M. van (1985). *Command in War*. Cambridge, MA: Harvard University Press.

Fromm, E. (1973). *The Anatomy of Human Destructiveness* (1973). New York: Holt Rinehart & Winston.

Gabriel, R.A. & Savage, P.L. (1979). *Crisis in Command. Mismanagement in the Army*. New York: Hill and Wang.

De Graaff, M.C., (2018). 'Morele krachten, de interpretatie van morele vraagstukken in militaire operaties.' *Militaire Spectator, 187*(7/8), 400–412.

De Graaff, M.C., Giebels, E. and Verweij, D.E.M. (2020). On moral grounds: Moral identity and moral disengagement in relation to military deployment. *Military Psychology, 32*(4), 363–375.

De Graaff, M.C. and Kramer, E.H. (2012). 'Leiderschap, uitzending en intelligent failure; de intelligente mislukking als hoeksteen van de lerende organisatie.' *M&O, Tijdschrift voor Management & Organisatie, Vol. 66*, No. 5, pp. 41–60.

Hackman, J.R., Oldham, G., Janson, R. and Purdy, K. (1975). A New Strategy for Job Enrichment. *California Management Review, 17*(4), 57–71.

Hersh, S. (2004). *Chain of Command: The Road from 9/11 to Abu Ghraib*. New York: Harper Collins.

Huntington, S.P. (1957). *The Soldier and the State: The Theory and Politics of Civil-Military Relations*. Cambridge, MA: The Belknap Press of Harvard University.

Isenberg, D. (1985). 'Some Hows and Whats of Managerial Thinking: Implications for Future Army Leaders.' In: J.G. Hunt and J.D. Blair (eds.). *Leadership on the Future Battlefield*. (pp. 168–181). Dulles, VA: Pergamon Brassey's.

Kaptein, M. (2008). Developing and testing a measure for the ethical culture of organizations: The corporate ethical virtues model. *Journal of Organizational Behavior: The International Journal of Industrial, Occupational and Organizational Psychology and Behavior, 29*(7), 923–947.

Kramer, E.H. (2007). *Organizing Doubt. Grounded Theory, Army Units and Dealing with Dynamic Complexity*. Copenhagen: Copenhagen Business University Press.

Kramer, E.H. and Kuipers, H. (2003). 'Flexibiliteit en starheid in krijgshistorisch perspectief.' *Militaire spectator*, Sept. 2003, pp. 454–471.

Kramer, E.H., Waard, E. de, Graaff, M. de (2012). 'Task Force Uruzgan and Experimentation with Organization Design.' In: Meulen, J. van der, Soeters, J., Beerens, R., Vogelaar, A. *Mission Uruzgan*. Amsterdam: Amsterdam University Press.

Kuipers, H. (1989). 'Zelforganisatie als ontwerpprincipe.' *Gedrag en Organisatie*, 2(4/5), pp. 199–221.

Kuipers, H., Amelsvoort, P. van, Kramer, E.H. (2020). *Het nieuwe organiseren: alternatieven voor de bureaucratie* (revised edition). Leuven: Acco.

Lifton, R.J. (1973). *Home from the War: Learning from Vietnam Veterans.* New York: Other Press.

Litz, B.T., Stein, N., Delaney, E., Lebowitz, L., Nash, W.P., Silva, C. and Maguen, S. (2009). 'Moral Injury and Moral Repair in War Veterans: A Preliminary Model and Intervention Strategy.' *Clin Psychol Rev* 29(8): 695–706. DOI: 10.1016/j.cpr.2009.07.003.

Lipsky, M. (1980). *Street-level Bureaucracy. Dilemmas of the Individual in Public Services.* New York: Russel Sage Foundation.

Molendijk, T. (2020). *Soldiers in Conflict. Moral Injury, Political Practices and Public Perceptions* (dissertation). Nijmegen: Radboud University.

Molendijk, T., Kramer, E-H., Verweij, D.E.M. (2018). 'Moral Aspects of 'Moral Injury': Analyzing Conceptualizations on the Role of Morality in Military Trauma.' *Journal of Military Ethics*, 17(1): 36–53.

Moorkamp, M. (2019). *Operating Under High-Risk Conditions in Temporary Organizations: A Sociotechnical Systems Perspective.* New York: Routledge.

Morgan, G. (2006). *Images of Organization* (2nd ed.). Thousand Oaks, CA: Sage.

Pick, D. (1993). *War Machine. The Rationalisation of Slaughter in the Modern Age.* New Haven: Yale University Press.

Shay, J. (1994). *Achilles in Vietnam.* New York: Scribner.

Sitter, L.U. de (2000). *Synergetisch produceren: Human Resources Mobilisation in de produktie. Een inleiding in structuurbouw.* Assen: Uitgeverij Van Gorcum (first edition 1994).

Stangneth, B. (2014). *Eichmann vor Jerusalem: Das unbehelligte Leben eines Massenmörders.* Hamburg: Rowohlt Verlag.

Swaan, A. de (2015). *The killing compartments. The Mentality of Mass Murder.* New Haven: Yale University Press.

Toulmin, S. (2001). *Return to Reason.* Cambridge, MA: Harvard University Press.

Trist, E.L., Higgin, G.W., Murray, H., Pollock, A.B. (1963). *Organizational Choice. Capabilities of Groups at the Coal Face Under Changing Technologies: The Loss, Rediscovery & Transformation of a Work Tradition.* London: Tavistock Publications.

Verkerk, M.J. (2004). *Trust and Power on the Shop Floor. An Ethnographical, Ethical and Philosophical Study of Responsible Behavior in Industrial Organizations.* Delft: Eburon.

Verweij, D. (2009). 'Denken in dialoog. Ethiek en de militaire praktijk.' *Militaire Spectator, 178*(1), pp. 15–25.

Visser, M. & Brouwer, J.J. (2007). 'Enkelslag in de veldslag: Organisatieleren onder condities van hiërarchie en discipline.' *M&O, 61*(5), 21–33.

Weick, K.E. (1979). *The Social Psychology of Organizing.* New York: McGraw-Hill.

Zimbardo, P. (2007). *The Lucifer Effect. Understanding how Good People Turn Evil.* New York: Random House.

CHAPTER 8

Morality

Foundation for Competent Professionals

G. J. van Doorn

1 Introduction

In this chapter it is argued that moral education (also called 'formation') within military organisations has a greater chance of success if we first describe the rather abstract concepts, ethics and morality, in concrete terms, and secondly, do so on the basis of a fundamental didactic notion, i.e. the layered structure of people's so-called 'competence household' (Van Doorn, 2019). This is relevant, because a lack of basic didactic knowledge may do more harm to moral education than promote it. The unintended outcome regularly makes it to the news media: serious wrongdoings in the practice of day-to-day task performance, at *all* levels of the organisation.

This chapter focusses on the following questions: What is *ethics*? (Section 2), What is *didactics*? (3), and (4): How can their *integration* contribute to moral education within the military? Based on real cases, we show how moral development is an elementary component of the training for competent military professionals. Finally, everyone is invited to reflect further on this in the *dialogue* section (5).

2 Ethics: Reflection on Morality

In this section we briefly examine the concepts of *ethics* (2.1) and *morality* (2.2), and address a major misunderstanding within this domain (2.3) with the help of four concrete case examples.[1]

---

1   The cases are based on actual facts and events and have been anonymised, thus making sure that the descriptions cannot be traced back to individuals or specific units. Sometimes the names of armed forces' divisions have also been deliberately changed. This is not about naming and shaming, but about the truthful representation of selected, real-life situations with instructional value, GJD.

MORALITY 101

2.1 *Ethics*

2.1.1 The General Concept of Ethics

As discussed in chapter 1, ethics is concerned with the critical reflection on our morality: a set of values and moral standards, the basic attitude forming the foundation for our daily conduct. The term dates back to the Ancient Greek ἦθος (nature, habit, character, personal disposition) and ἠθικός (related to morals).

Ethical issues are either descriptive or prescriptive; the former more theoretical, the latter more practical in nature, about the 'rightness' or 'wrongness' of our actions and the criteria against which to measure them. According to the Sophists however, the concepts of 'good' and 'evil' lacked universal validity (Giannopoulou, 2009). Conversely, Socrates (469–399 BC), through Plato (427–347 BC), argued that absolute virtue was in fact possible, if only someone had the right 'in-house knowledge', meaning … of *himself*. Immoral action does not arise from malicious intent, but from ignorance. Aristotle (384–322 BC), for his part, qualified this: even if someone *knows* that a particular action is wrong, he may still proceed, 'against better judgment' (Destrée 2007).

2.1.2 Types of Ethics in Brief

In the *descriptive* approach to ethics, morality is regarded as an actual basis for observable behaviour, without taking a normative stand towards it. Important questions are: What beliefs do people have, and how deeply rooted are they within specific groups? What are the underlying values? How explicitly do people articulate these values, or do they act solely on the basis of tacit assumptions?

In the *prescriptive* approach, someone takes a normative stand towards morality, and presents arguments for the defence thereof (see also Chapter 2). A three-way distinction is commonly made between (1) ethics of *duty*, (2) ethics of *consequence* and (3) *virtue* ethics (see also chapter 2). The ethics of *duty* measures someone's soundness based on the correctness of his actions: these can only be 'intrinsically good' (Alexander & Moore, 2015), if so is the *intended* goal (Gaus, 2001) (hence also: *intentional ethics*; Weber & Gillespie, 1998). The ethics of *consequence* assesses a person's reliability in terms of the ultimate effect of his actions, the goal *achieved* (George & Johnson, 1985) (also: *result* or *outcome ethics*; Neher & Sandin, 2017). The latter is often described in contrast to the former, but the two need not be mutually exclusive (Vallentyne, 1987).

As discussed in chapter 2, *virtue* ethics focuses neither on the intentions nor the outcomes of our actions (Hacker-Wright, 2010), so much more rather on our disposition. According to Socrates, we need to shift our attention from the outside world to our inner world (Marton & Booth, 2013). He labelled self-knowledge 'of the highest order', all other – secular – knowledge being secondary (Moore, 2015). He who knows 'what is right' from within, will naturally do 'the right thing' in the outside world. According to Aristotle, rational development was paramount for this: (cognitive) self-awareness distinguishes mankind from the animal world (Angier, 2010).

As its name already suggests, the field of *applied ethics* seeks to apply theoretical moral principles to everyday practical situations (Beauchamp, 2003a; see also chapter 1). According to James (Barbalet, 1997) and Dewey (Fesmire, 2003) however, moral action is less based on rational considerations, rather than on lived-through experiences, within the context of one's own community (Koopman, 2009). Central to this is the human need for clarity: we seem to feel more comfortable with quite a simplified, *dual-faceted* display of the situation, preferably in terms of extremes, i.e. as dichotomies (Collier & Adcock, 1999). Moral issues, however, are usually *multi-faceted*; handling them skilfully therefore requires a multiple perspective. The answer to the 'key question' only rarely will be a simple 'right' or 'wrong'. In the same vein, moral dilemmas require nuanced presentation, followed by ditto judgment and decision-making (Collinson, 2014).

As discussed in chapter 1, military ethics is a typical example of *applied ethics*, similar to *medical ethics*. In both variants, the problem of double loyalty frequently arises (Coleman, 2009; see also Chapter 4) and split-second decisions must often be made, sometimes about life and death (as discussed in many of the previous chapters; see also Van Baarle, 2018).

2.2 *Morality*

2.2.1 The General Concept of Morality

Morality (Lat., *moralitas*: character, virtue; *mores*: manners, suitable conduct) is the field of inquiry in which human action is judged as 'appropriate' (vs. inappropriate) or 'desirable' (vs. undesirable) (see chapter 1). Human behaviour is called 'moral' if it is 'right', 'immoral' if it is 'wrong' (Milo, 2014), and 'amoral' if at any rate it evades any discussion on morality.

As discussed in chapter 1, morality may differ considerably between populations, but also exhibit similarities. A distinction is often made between *universal* (Evanoff, 2004) and *relative* (Fassin, 2014) morality. The former is *always* present, in *all* cultures, with virtues such as frugality, humanity, courage, justice and wisdom (Beauchamp, 2003b; see also chapter 1). The latter varies according to place, time and circumstances (Shweder, 2012; Westermarck, 1932, 2017): what is considered morally acceptable in one society may just as well be immoral in another (Westacott, 2015). Critics of this so-called *moral*

MORALITY 103

relativism argue that genocide, slavery and child abuse should not be ignored out of 'respect for local circumstances and traditions' (Wong, 2016).

2.2.2 Values and Standards

Ethics as a dynamic field of operations concerns the critical reflection on our 'moral housekeeping' or 'household':[2] our combined set of values and moral standards. As discussed in chapter 1, values are the things in life we consider important, the so-called 'ideals' or 'higher goals' (Eccles & Wigfield, 2002). They are fundamental and fairly universal (Vauclair, Wilson & Fischer, 2014), usually stable, change little over time (Rokeach, 2008), and are therefore less susceptible to influence by learning processes (Van Doorn & Lingsma, 2019). Examples are reliability, collegiality, flexibility, loyalty, and dedication.

Also discussed in chapter 1, standards (norms) are the guidelines for our actions (Railton, 2003), bridging the gap between the abstract values and our much more concrete, observable behaviour (Lönnqvist, Walkowitz, Wichardt, Lindeman & Verkasalo, 2009). These rules of conduct are sometimes written or even prescribed, sometimes unwritten, and in general broadly accepted socially. Additionally, they tend to change more over time (Godecharle, Nemery & Dierickx, 2014), and may vary according to society, (sub)culture or social class (Sverdlik, Roccas & Sagiv, 2012). Within these environments, deviating behaviour is often not accepted, as a consequence of which it falls prey to adjustments to an apparently agreed standard; sometimes mildly, by subtle reprimand, sometimes more firmly, by punishment or even group exclusion (Killen, Rutland, Abrams, Mulvey & Hitti, 2013). Examples are keeping to speed limits within built-up areas and not jumping queues.

Verweij (2000) compares the ethics domain with a pyramid. In this model, introspective reflection aims to focus from above upon (1) the moral standards, and (2) the underlying values, as in Figure 8.1.

Figure 8.1 shows how ethics encompasses the whole: the critical reflection upon the *complex* of our moral standards and values. The figure also makes clear that moral standards 'only work if they are based on values' (Verweij, 2010; see also chapter 1). For example, the speed limit of 30 km/h is based on the values of *road safety* and *social responsibility*.

In Section 4 – on the relationship between ethics and didactics – we show that the top-down reflection on moral standards and values within Verweij's

---

2   The first term seems to suggest more of a process, the second rather a solidified situation. The latter might make the reader feel unfairly misled, because it is precisely *the dynamics* within someone's 'intra-personal system' onto which explorative and interventional actions focus their attention, GJD.

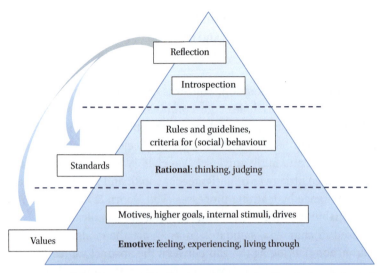

FIGURE 8.1 The ethics pyramid; reflection upon morality: Standards and the underlying values, as foundation for our action

pyramid follows the same layered structure as the bottom-up action motivated by emotions and reasoning in McClelland's 'iceberg model' (depicting the didactics domain). Thus, we may come to understand that *reflective practitioning* (Van Doorn, 2019) is 'nothing but' constantly asking ourselves (*reflective*) which values (primarily affective) and norms (cognitive) form the basis for our behaviour (operative), in order to convert this into new, (self)insightful action (*practitioning*) in daily reality. We will elaborate on this picture further in said section.

2.2.3   Morality and Integrity

The integral concept of morality implies that *integrity* is a hallmark of virtuous action. This is not surprising, as both 'integral' and 'integrity' are derived from the Latin *integritas*: intactness, wholeness, completeness; *integer*: flawless, unimpaired, entire. Derived from this is the verb *integrare*: to merge into one whole. Someone with integrity acts congruently with his views and beliefs (standards) and the things he considers important (values) (Storr, 2004). This consistent attitude lends him credibility and reliability, regardless of place, time and circumstances. Furthermore, he is not corrupt (Lat., *corrumpere*: tear apart, violate), because he is not torn by internal conflicts or by external conflicts between himself and his interlocutor(s) (Pardo, 2015).[3] In

---

3 This does not mean that a person of integrity cannot feel torn by having to choose between two evils, as in a so-called 'tragic moral dilemma'. Several authors (e.g. Cox, La Caze & Levine,

MORALITY

addition, *transparency* is often mentioned as an important characteristic of leaders of integrity (Vogelgesang, Leroy & Avolio, 2013): they have no hidden agenda (Schipper, 2016). When someone pays lip service to 'norms and values' and then flouts them, this is called (moral) hypocrisy (Naso, 2006). Managers often violate their – professed – moral standards while pursuing their own – alleged – self-interest (Grant, 2008; Maner & Mead, 2010).

2.3 *A Major Misconception of Morality*

A notable misunderstanding is the idea that loyalty to the organisation is at odds with being loyal to yourself or your colleagues (also referred to as dual loyalty[4]) (see also chapter 4). When deployed, soldiers have to act 'as instructed', but when doing so, they often come into conflict with their own conscience. Below we set the scenes of four real-life situations, followed by some questions for reflection.

Case 1 – Father and son at the main gate …

Sergeant Major X is the staff guard's platoon commander at Camp Holland in Uruzgan, in charge of security and access control at the main gate. Right behind the gate, the logistics supplies are kept in a refrigerated container. According to instructions, these supplies – combat rations, water, etc. – are intended solely for own military personnel; under no circumstances may any of the resources be provided to locals.

One morning, an Afghan man arrives at the gate with his four-year-old son, who is clearly starving. The sergeant major has three children of his own in the Netherlands and feels 'that children should not want for anything'. Despite the strict guidelines, he decides to admit father and son to the camp, and orders one of his troops to provide them with sufficient food and water.

2003) have shown that feeling doubt in such a situation is *indeed* a sign of integrity. A single focus on one's *own* values and moral standards means that the requirement of *contextual awareness* (i.e. the first critical success factor for coaching; Van Doorn & Lingsma, 2019) is not met. Integrity therefore has both an internal and an external meaning (or: intra-individual and supra-individual); the latter requires professionals to be aware of and sensitive to the interests of the other people involved, and to do justice to these. From an *integral* – or: holistic – systems perspective (Van Doorn, 2021), an exclusively inward-looking approach is a fragmented one, and therefore not associated with integrity. The effects of such an approach can be very destructive.

4 In terms of the five critical success factors for coaching (CSF) – this issue arises when there is an unmanageable tension between someone's external system (Context, CSF-1) and his internal system (Iceberg, CSF-4), GJD.

In this case example we may ask a number of (self-)reflective questions in the context of moral action:

- If the goal of the mission is 'help rebuild a society with a population in need', what can we say about Sergeant Major X's superior – Captain C – who severely reprimands him, after discovering his 'inappropriate initiative', warning him to 'never do this again'?
- What is going on here, in terms of standards, duty performance and commitment to people in need?
- What should be the deciding factor here?[5]

Case 2 – Loyal buddy ...

Sergeant Y is a section commander on deployment in Mali, an NCO with a good reputation, who has received many commendations. He is now doing his dream job: leading a section in a recce platoon. He is known for his loyalty to his men. This is a must, he believes: without loyalty there can be no group bonding, while that is the very basis for teamwork. He always wanted to be a soldier, it's 'what he lives for' ...

One day, Sergeant Z – fellow section commander and his buddy since the Royal Military NCOs' School –, comes to him with 'some exciting news'. During a patrol, he (Z) 'had his way with a local woman' and the sex was awesome! He is quite proud of this feat and advises Y to pay her a visit too on his next patrol. Sergeant Y smiles, and only tells Z to watch out for diseases. Of course, he's not going to report his buddy's behaviour to their PC: 'He's my buddy, and we've got each other's back no matter what ...'

Also in this case example we may ask a number of (self-)reflective questions:

- In terms of morality, what values and standards are at stake here?
- Can Z's behaviour be justified by reference to moral relativism (2.2)?
- If Y – after much deliberation – decides to report this incident to the PC after all, what argument can he use, without risking immediately being blamed for being a snitch?

---

5 In the dialogue section we will elaborate on these types of questions in more detail, without providing a pre-conceived answer. However, it is useful to draw attention to the potential effects of certain choices. 'Giving food once' may, for instance, set an undesirable precedent, whereby several fathers and sons may appear at the gate the next day to be fed. On the other hand, if you do not provide food, how great is the risk that the local population will collectively turn against you?

MORALITY

Case 3 – Booking and cleaning up ...

Chora, Afghanistan. Lieutenant A's job is to register and check incoming detainees. He has studied the rules of interrogation and knows that detainees may not be physically 'encouraged' to talk. So no threats of physical violence, and certainly no use of it. Today he has registered a young detainee who is then taken away by two interrogators. One of them is his superior, who also reviews his performance; a 'nice chap', widely praised for being a 'role model' ...

This is A's first position in the interrogation unit and he's loving it; he would like to make a career in the world of intelligence. That's where he sees his future, and the INTELL work is so much more exciting than his previous jobs in logistics.

After an hour, the interrogators return. They ask A to 'clean up the mess in the interrogation room' and to feed the detainee. Upon entering, A sees the detainee's blood-smeared face, and he is unconscious. He brings him around and cleans his face. After tidying up the room, he continues his work: registering and checking prisoners ...

In this case example we may ask the following (self-)reflective questions:
- What values and moral standards are at odds with each other here?
- What is at the heart of the 'internal conflict' that A might be facing here?
- What should the deciding factor be here?
- Which argument has most weight, and why?

Case 4 – You cannot help everyone ...

During the war in Bosnia (1990s) a seven-year-old boy is shot in the head and dies on the spot. His mother is wounded and severely traumatised by the events. As an SFOR soldier, Captain B, is involved in this firing incident, albeit indirectly. Together with his sergeant major he decides to help the single mother and her other two children in whatever way possible. But, SFOR does not wish to become involved in 'such private help initiatives'. It forbids him to support the woman: 'This is a drop in the ocean, and you cannot help everyone ...'

Despite the order, the captain and the sergeant major decide to donate as much money and food as possible as well as all kinds of 'surplus items'. Making use of SFOR resources, they ensure the woman is given better accommodation and her deceased son a fine tombstone. A few years later, a small yet dignified monument is inaugurated at the scene of the incident.

In this case example, an infinite number of (self-)reflective questions can be asked. A selection:

- B's action is in line with the notion of 'helping a population in need'. Nevertheless, SFOR leadership soon afterwards officially announces that 'from now on, initiatives of this kind will no longer be condoned'. Between which two loyalties are soldiers thus forced to choose?
- Is B's 'unauthorised action' a matter of ethics of *duty* or ethics of *consequence*?
- Provide arguments in favour of B's decision to proceed with his 'inappropriate initiative'.

Acting with integrity (1) cannot be based on a 'loose set of standards' (2) while the underlying values (3) are unknown or even missing. How these three levels – doing, thinking and motivation – relate to each other from a didactic point of view will be discussed in the next section.

3   Didactics: Training for Competent Action

In this section we look at the specific field of knowledge and skills transfer: didactics (3.1). A central role is played by the threefold layered structure of the (integral) concept of competence (3.2). With the help of four concrete case examples, we focus on a number of misunderstandings that may seriously disrupt learning, both the process as well as its produce (3.3).

3.1   *Didactics*

Didactics-as-method is often mentioned together with *dialectics* and the method of *critical thinking*. After discussing these below, we zero in on the concept of 'relevant knowledge'.

3.1.1   Didactics, Dialectics and the Method of Critical Thinking

Didactics (Gr., διδάσκειν: teaching, training) concerns the process of presenting relevant information to learners. Professional literature emphasises the art of *instruction*, aimed at improving performance; so-called 'literary' literature sometimes also contains moral elements (Hamm, 1940).

Dialectics (Gr., διάλεκτική: conducting a dialogue) is a conversation method in which two or more participants take different positions on a particular subject and attempt to find out the truth together through logical reasoning (Davidson, 1994; Baxter & Montgomery, 1996). The distinction with traditional didactics lies in the equal standing of the interlocutors. In didactics, one (the active party) teaches the other (the passive party); an *opposing discussion* is held in which the participants (who are subjective, partial) put forward the

MORALITY 109

correctness of their own point of view and rhetorically fight each other with arguments (Worthington, 2010).

In dialectics, both interlocutors search for a missing insight *together*: an *investigative dialogue* is held about an event or circumstance (objective, neutral), without one trying to convince the other. In order for learners to gain their own insights, it is important that *discussion* makes way for *dialogue*, and speaking for listening. This requires a shift in the role of their supervisors (Pedler, 2011).

Listening is also more important than speaking in the *method of critical thinking*. In Plato's dialogues (Stokes, 1986) Socrates demanded a critical attitude from his interlocutors (Gr., κριτήριον: standard, measure; κριτικός: capable of making a distinction). He warned that for developing our awareness it is better not to rely on people who are vested with any 'authority'. Even though such people may occupy positions of great power and prestige, they often appear to be extremely confused and irrational (Williams & Shepard, 1995). He therefore argued that one should not accept their ideas blindly but ask in-depth questions instead, before trusting them (Colaiaco, 2013). The aim was to arrive at 'true statements' through valid reasoning, rather than falling prey to fundamental fallacies and credulity (Herrick, 2015). In essence, critical thinking entails ceaselessly challenging established beliefs, by carefully examining underlying assumptions and always demanding sound reasoning from conversation partners (Ennis, 1987).

3.1.2 The Relationship between Worldly Knowledge and Self-knowledge

The three approaches (didactics, dialectics, and critical thinking) differ in (1) their appreciation of what relevant knowledge is, and (2) the way in which this can be acquired. Didactics provides knowledge and is mainly 'externally driven' (*teacher-centred*). In dialectics, interlocutors conduct the discovery dialogue together in search of knowledge (*content and process-centred*). The critical thinking method aims to unlock the knowledge someone has available naturally, thus being mainly 'internally fed' (*learner-centred*).

Gordon (1996) emphasises the moral dimension of dialectics and dialogue (as with Socrates and Plato), because self-discovery benefits the clarity of one's own perception, and thus the soundness of one's own actions. The old Greek adage γνῶθι σεαυτόν (know thyself) gained prominence through Socrates' core idea that knowledge of the world is not possible without self-knowledge. This explains his incessant plea for critical (self-)reflection, including a serious contemplation of one's own motives (Moore, 2015). In his view, there is no use whatsoever in exploring things *outside* ourselves, as long as we have not yet taken notice *of* ourselves (Griswold, 1981). To summarise: unless and until

I become aware of the filters that obscure my pure perception of the outside world, it will be useless to focus on the latter. All I know for sure is that this image will be distorted. And because those filters are part of *myself*, my first task is to *examine myself*, so that I learn how they work, and blur my outward view (Griswold Jr., 2010). If I want to live a successful, virtuous life, I must first and foremost get to know myself, before I face the world (Moore, 2014).

3.2 The Layered Concept of Competence

Socrates' self-concept – the integrated personality – is very similar to the integral concept of competence that we use when guiding learning processes (Kraiger, Ford & Salas, 1993). To accurately portray its layered structure (Spencer & Spencer, 1993), we use McClelland's iceberg metaphor (McClelland, 1998). A competence is: 'the combination of (operative) skills and (cognitive and affective) attitudinal aspects that must be used in the execution of a job or set of tasks, such that the performance meets the requirements as stipulated by the professional group to which a person belongs' (Van Doorn & Lingsma 2019, p. 219). Figure 8.2 shows everything in a single overview.

Figure 8.2 shows that effective functioning presupposes constant alignment between the three layers within a person's 'iceberg'. Acting congruently means: in accordance with one's own thoughts and feelings (Sheldon & Kasser, 1995). Above the waterline our behaviour is observable, but our thoughts and feelings are not, since they are located underneath. Yet it is precisely these invisible elements that nourish our visible actions. In this, the waterline exactly fulfils the function of Socrates' filter between the lower and the upper current, thus preventing us from seeing which cognitions and affects do in fact cause our behaviour. In didactic terms: anyone who does not get to know himself as an integrated human being (not only his *actions*, but especially his *thoughts* and *motives*), will not be capable of competent action, because it inevitably remains fragmented. In ethical terms: anyone who does not ask himself – through critical self-reflection – *what* he does, *how* and *how well* he does it (standards) and *why* he does it (values *to begin with*; see also: Van Doorn, 2021), fails to look after his own integrity.

3.3 A Few Misunderstandings about Moral Education

Up to this day, many trainers still use a teacher-centred approach to their task. This may still be understandable at the level of *craftsmanship*, which mainly involves the appropriation of external skills (operative): the senior steers the junior through the process of learning the trade.[6] However, at the level of

---

6 Compare *mentoring* and *coaching*: *subject matter-specific* versus *process* guidance; GJD.

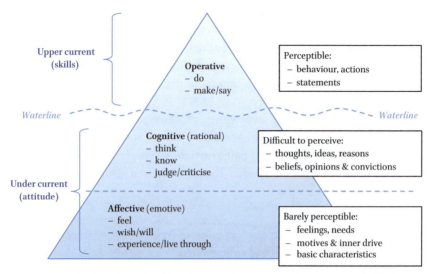

FIGURE 8.2 The three-layered Iceberg: Operative (upper current), cognitive and affective (under current)

self-in-relation-to-own-task-or-function 'learning from someone else' is *essentially not possible*, since this is all about internal thoughts and feelings, the learner's personal features or traits (cognitive and affective). From Socrates to Rogers (1947) and long since then, thinkers about personal development have emphasised: the only expert in the field of a person's characteristics is ... *the learner himself* (Joseph, 2006). Hence, *moral education* – below the waterline – pre-eminently calls for a learner-centred approach. The trainer who tells learners 'how to behave' is not educating them, but forces them into certain actions. In that case, there is no healthy teacher-student relationship, but sheer abuse of power ... Cases 5 to 7 contain some poignant examples.[7]

3.3.1   Thinking That for You as a Trainer It's Enough to Utter a Few Slogans ...

Case 5 – The angry captain: personal development and discipline clearly mistaken ...

Breda, The Netherlands, mid-2019. The captain, responsible for training at the Royal Military Academy, was angry, no ... *furious*! Those young lads

---

7 The cases have been numbered consecutively for easy reference during classes, GJD.

'had no idea anymore what discipline was'. And there, in the other building, 'at the Faculty with those armchair experts', 'no attention at all was given to *personal development*!' When asked for an example, he thought briefly and said: 'They don't even have to report the class to the teacher before instruction and there's no saluting anymore ...' All respect 'had totally disappeared' ...

In his days they wouldn't get away with that ... shoes polished and trousers creased, that's what it was about ... And if they weren't, you got a "shove"[8] ... You just knew where you stood ... 'being on time, do what you're told, standards and values, that sort of thing ...' The captain had a very intense look on his face as he spoke.

In this case example, we can ask a number of (self-)reflective questions from the perspective of the concept of competence:
– What concept of 'discipline' might this captain be relying on?
– What, in his opinion, does 'personal development' mean?
– If you were to ask him what 'standards and values' are, what would he possibly answer?

Discipline etymologically means: *learning* (Lat., *disciplina* [knowledge; instruction] and *discipulus* [learner; pupil]; from *discernere*: learn, distinguish [Van Veen & Van der Sijs, 1997]) and *docere*: teach, instruct, train [Onions, Friedrichsen & Burchfield, 1966]). Adopting a definition in the narrow sense of the word[9] (do as you're told; obedience) most certainly would lead to a misnomer, for it does not entirely capture the gist of the term. A broader, more appropriate translation would be: capability or propensity for learning.

3.3.2 Thinking That You're Engaged in 'Moral Education' by Setting Standards and Enforcing Compliance

Case 6 – The resolute sergeant major: I teach by example ...

Breda 2018, the Netherlands. The cheerful, portly sergeant major 'liked a beer' and 'loved a good meal'. But, he was quick to add, that did not mean he did not take his job seriously! When asked how he saw his own task, he said: '... to show the young cadets how to do it', by 'setting the right example'. For example, the obligation to salute taught them to show respect for

---

8 Slang for martial or disciplinary punishment.
9 Typically and possibly quite telling: the word for *narrow* in Dutch (which is 'eng') also means 'scary' or 'frightening', GJD.

MORALITY   113

those higher in rank, they learned to conform to traditions and to comply with dress regulations. The question 'Where should all this lead to?' was at first met with silence ...

When asked whether he thought he was achieving the desired result with his approach to 'moral education', he suddenly became very resolute. He referred to a booklet on 'the exemplary role', which stated plainly that 'behaviour was the starting point', and that this 'required clear rules and regulations'. Quotation: 'As in parenting, it starts with setting the standard and then developing awareness of the underlying value.'

The booklet stated that 'behaviour is the starting point' for personal development (Netherlands Defence Academy Staff 2017, p. 6). However, this is evidently about *desired* behaviour; it is therefore *not* the starting point, but the *purpose* of the so-called 'formation' ... Then it says on the same page (...) that 'as in parenting, moral education begins with setting the *standard*' (italics added). These contradictory statements reveal serious confusion about both the morality and the competence concept. After all: moral education *begins* with identifying a value, on the basis of which standards and desired, job-related behaviour can then ensue, logically and understandably (Sinek, 2009).

This case example also allows us to ask ourselves a number of (self-)reflective questions:

– How can we train future leaders to become self-directed learners, if the 'precept' for this is based so evidently on a number of fundamental misconceptions?
– How does a 'pronounced exemplary role' relate to 'respect for the learner'?

3.3.3 Considering Yourself an 'Expert' in the Field of Other People's Personal Development ...

Case 7 – The magnificent lieutenant colonel ...

He started out as a sergeant long ago, so 'he knew the score'. Now he had become an *Advisor on Personal Development* at the Operational Command,[10] advising and assisting unit commanders during exercises in issues concerning the 'formation' of troops into 'good soldiers'. He had a very earnest look on his face, as if it were a matter of utmost seriousness ...

---

10   Operational Commands: RNLAF (Air Force), RNLN (Navy), RNLA (Army) and RNLMP (Military Police).

When asked what he meant by 'formation', he verbosely explained that it was all about 'applying rules and regulations', 'enforcing compliance to standards and values', 'obeying superiors' and 'adhering to strict discipline', 'things like that'. ... As an NCO, he had come to understand the great benefits of these concepts. He treasured his years of experience as a scout, was 'proud of it'... Now he was determined to pass on his knowledge to others ...

In this case example, we may again ask a number of (self) reflective questions:

- From where or what does the Defence organisation derive its apparently implicit concept of 'personal development'?
- What is it that keeps our organisation from formulating this concept explicitly, so that we all understand what we are talking about before we start discussing it?
- How is it possible that the relationship between ethics (moral education) and didactics (competence training) has remained underexposed for so long in an organisation that empathically puts 'character formation' on the agenda, repeatedly and with quite some fanfare?
- What might be the effect of having someone with 'a great deal of experience' (*external*) in the position of an advisor on matters of *personal development*, whereas it is precisely the *internal household of the learner himself* that has to be examined, discovered and well-kept?

The next section deals with the combination of ethics and didactics, respectively concerning our *integrity and competence management*, or *household*. The idea of *housekeeping* implies that you have to maintain something in its entirety: you must keep sight of it, keep it clean (pure) and functioning, and repair it when it has shortcomings or even serious defects. You also occasionally let someone else have a look at it, and you allow yourself some guidance, either by peers or by a professional (Van Doorn & Lingsma, 2013). Important to realise in all of this: you are and will remain *the* expert on your own personal architecture and design. There can only be one, naturally ...

4 Ethics and Didactics: Moral Reflection as a Basis for Competent Action

In this section we bring together the essence of ethics and didactics under one heading (4.1), and give an example of how a persistent misunderstanding can also be solved (4.2).

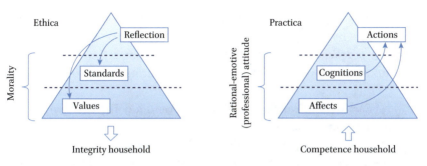

FIGURE 8.3 The ethics pyramid and the didactics iceberg: Reflection upon morality and action based on professional attitude

4.1 *The Inextricable Relationship between Action and Reflection*

The combination of ethics (aiming at moral self-awareness) and didactics (aiming at competent action) has its basis in Aristotle's dyad ETHICA–PRACTICA. Aristotle regarded ethics as a practical discipline, focusing on the (virtuous) functioning of man. In his eyes, it was not enough 'to fathom ethical issues superficially' (Aristotle, 2014). He advocated a comprehensive, non-relative doctrine of virtues (Nussbaum, 1993), in which both rational considerations and emotions had their place (Nussbaum, 1996). Figure 8.3 shows how the ethics and didactics metaphor (see Sections 1 and 2) can be combined to form a single, yet two-pronged mode of reflecting (ethically) and acting (practically).

Figure 8.3 shows that the integrity household (left) and the competence household (right) have the shape of a pyramid or an iceberg.[11] The first depicts the reflection, the downward introspection of the standards and values underneath. A regular 'integrity check-up' enables us to better understand ourselves in terms of *morality*. The second illustrates the upward nurturing of manifest behaviour above the waterline; from the undermost level of experienced affects, via the cognitions just up there. A sound 'competence build-up' enables us to perform congruently, according to a solid, reliable *rational-emotive professional attitude*.

The combination of these two movements gives substance to the process of *reflective practitioning*: asking yourself *what* you are doing, *how* and *why* (becoming aware of your fundamental values), and acting on the basis of your

---

11 Both constructs are widest at their base, and with good reason: if the base were narrower – as with a cube – the middle and top layers would be less firmly sustained, and might start wobbling, or even topple over. The values (affects) support the standards (cognitions), and together they support the actions. Hence: morality as *foundation* for competent professionals.

own feelings and thoughts[12] (operating with self-awareness). In the left-hand model, *ethical reflection* on one's own morality takes place, in the right-hand model the *practical action* ensuing from that. Top-down (inward) reflection and bottom-up (outward) action thus form one continuous, circular process.

4.2 *A Persistent Misunderstanding That Eventually Tasted Defeat ...*

A common misunderstanding is to think that you promote professionalism in your organisation by simply prescribing behaviour. Worse still, this misconception is not limited to 'the shop floor', but is especially persistent among politicians and administrators, as the following case example shows.

Case 8 – The vigorous inspector ... prescribed behaviour ...

In 1998, the then Inspector General of the Netherlands Armed Forces slated the so-called 'Code of Conduct for Defence Personnel' in his annual report. It was allegedly *far too general* (italics mine, GJD), as a result of which there was 'no clear and practicable system of rules of conduct in the workplace '. That made it too difficult 'to work with it in everyday practice'.

Two years earlier, the MOD had announced with some ruffles and flourishes that it was to 'increase the professionalism of the soldiers by means of a set of rules of conduct'. Much to the great disappointment of the armed forces' middle management – but particularly of many MPs in the House of Representatives – the new code ultimately turned out not to go any further than a number of very general guidelines. This would make 'too small the enforceability of the desired behaviour'.

What was going on here, from the perspective of the *integral concept of competence*? If we define professionalism as 'performing competently' (in terms of McClelland's iceberg: acting, thinking *and* feeling; in terms of Verweij's pyramid: through reflection on our standards *and* values), it becomes clear that prescribing a set of behaviours is a recipe for 'truncated functioning'; as a

---

12   Note: acting 'on the basis on one's own feelings and thoughts' is not yet *per se* morally correct. A criminal does so too, but usually ignores the interests of others, or even deliberately harms them. Integrity must – in the context of corporate training – meet the requirement of internal and external consistency (Kessels & Harrison, 1998; Kessels & Plomp, 1999), and, in terms of guiding learning processes, the requirement of internal *and* external systems orientation (Van Doorn & Lingsma, 2019).

MORALITY 117

disabled person, rather than someone well-equipped. After all, the – literally *pre*-conditional – affects and cognitions are lacking. The accursed 'very general guidelines' in fact allowed more room for integral, professional functioning than the – detailed instructional – rules of conduct that were being advocated. It would have been better for the standard-bearers of such rules to ask: how can we ensure that our people will exhibit the 'desired behaviour'? And we are back to the professional domain of … integrative didactics.

Acting professionally, i.e. *respons*-ibly, means that you can – at any time – *respond* to the threefold question '*What* exactly are you doing, *how* do you do this, and *why*?' (Van Doorn & Lingsma, 2019). Here again we recognise the 'iceberg triad', deliberately designed and filled in upwards, for educational purposes ('start with the why'; Sinek, 2009). In daily practice – during our work activities – we reflect downwards on our task notions (norms or standards) and work motivation (underlying values) via the 'pyramid triad'. Applying the thus gained (self-)insight into new actions is an ongoing, circular process, as outlined with the two-fold composite Figure 8.3.

Seen from this perspective, the current, recently revised code of conduct (2017)[13] is therefore … *much better*! It describes 'only' the four basic values that are meaningful to the MOD, and from which professional performance should follow logically and comprehensibly: (1) connectedness, (2) safety and security, (3) trust, (4) responsibility. The explanation given to each of these has not led to a (renewed) set of rigidly prescribed rules, but leaves room for personal growth and development of each learner, according to his or her learning requirements or needs. So we *can* do it …

5   Dialogue

In this section we invite everyone to further reflect on the cases submitted above, by deliberately asking open questions instead of advancing propositions. We do not aim to draw conclusions here, but look for the continuous, dialectical conversation or dialogue. After all, we want to move from *old-school* didactics (teacher-centred) to *new-school* critical thinking (learner-centred), which leaves room for learners to make their *own* discoveries … So we do not tell 'how to', but ask ourselves: what can the actors involved – with a little more ethical and didactic (self-)knowledge – do differently from now on, perhaps even better?

---

13   Last retrieved January 17, 2020, from: https://www.defensie.nl.

Case 1: Father and Son at the Main Gate

How can the combination of ethics and didactics help us deal with this dilemma carefully? The sergeant major remained faithful to his own value 'consideration to the needs of the vulnerable', while the captain applied 'the standards imposed from higher up'. What conversation might they possibly have had, had it been based on the realisation that professional action can only be labelled 'competent' if 'the requirement of morality' had been met? What would their joint *reflective practitioning* (Sections 2 and 4) have looked like?

Case 2: Loyal Buddy

What ... if this time we do *not* jump to a conclusion? What does the difference in Sergeant Y's and Sergeant Z's situations – one from the theory of detached reflection, the other amidst the practice of close temptation – mean for their analysis and justification of their actions? Which ethical-didactical insights would have kept Z from having sex with a local woman, and would have prompted Y to bring this up for discussion? What is 'acting appropriately' in this dilemma of dual loyalty (Section 2)?

Case 3: Booking and Cleaning Up

Would it have made any difference if the immediate superior and the lieutenant had realised that 'professionalism' means that you can always answer the threefold question (1) *what* are you doing? (2) *why* are you doing it? and (3) *why* exactly are you doing it *this way*? These are the three layers of our competence household; reflection on the latter two concerns our moral housekeeping. Functioning congruently (Section 3) means to act in accordance with one's own thoughts (standards) and feelings (values). What might conscious reflection on this event (Sections 2 and 4) lead to?

Case 4: You Cannot Help Everyone

The captain was repeatedly summoned to stop 'such private help initiatives', but let his personal values prevail over the standards of the organisation (based on which values?). Moral courage of an individual, humane employee within a mechanical, dehumanised organisation? How is it possible that on the two levels there is *non-alignment* of the ideas about professionalism and competent action (Van Doorn, 2017), the latter being

MORALITY 119

inherently moral by its very nature? How can we prevent our personnel from being confronted with an impossible choice between two 'conflicting loyalties'?[14]

Case 5: The Angry Captain

If ...

1. moral education has *nothing whatsoever* to do with plain, one-dimensional behavioural instructions (the mere *'what'*) such as 'saluting superiors' or 'reporting to a teacher', and if ...
2. moral education *does* indeed take place below McClelland's water-line, at the level of task notions and work motivation (the *'how and why'*; see Figure 8.2; in terms of Verweij's pyramid: the standards and the values, Figure 8.1) ...

how might then this captain have successfully promoted 'his' formational goals (notably *the why*) in a didactically proficient manner?

Case 6: The Resolute Sergeant Major

If ...

1. 'learning from another person' is only possible at skills level, i.e. above McClelland's waterline (Section 3), and if ...
2. 'moral education' takes place below it, because this concerns a person's *personal* relationship to his task and motivation, and if ...
3. influencing someone's behaviour is thus not *personal development* (or: *'formation'*), but simply *instruction* (giving a compulsory order, aimed at the correct execution of skills & drills)

then, what does this really mean for the 'exemplary role' so often advocated, or for the propagation of 'role models'? And: how does this relate to the call for 'authenticity' that is also often heard?

Case 7: The Magnificent Lieutenant Colonel

Now, what about a lieutenant colonel who is mainly mistaken about ... *himself*? Because if ...

---

14 As in Case 1, we may ask ourselves whether this can always be prevented. See also the footnote about 'feeling torn between two evils' in Section 3.2, under the heading *Morality and integrity*.

1. 'transferring your own experience to the other person' is *not* the way to help him, and if ...
2. your outer (behavioural) experience is *not* what he needs, because his inner (rational-emotive) formation can only properly be served by a *descent into himself*; Sections 2 and 3), and if ...
3. 'offering one's own experience to others' is more a sign of a self-righteous ego overestimating himself, rather than genuine respect for the learner ...

then, who at all is going to coach this *personal development advisor*?

6   Epilogue

6.1   *Moral Education: A Never-ending Circular Process*

In this chapter we showed how moral education is a foundational element – also literally – of the training of competent professionals. To this end, the *integration of ethics and didactics* is an important prerequisite. Our integrity household reveals how we reflect on our personal morality, consisting of standards and values, while our competence household gives substance to our actions, based on our professional attitude, shaped by our thoughts and feelings (see Figure 8.3).

Acting and reflecting as such may be person- and profession-specific, but in a general sense they can indeed be influenced by means of learning processes. Morally responsible job behaviour may be (further) developed by paying attention to precisely this *combination of task performance (practice)* and a *continuous critical observation* thereof (*reflection*).

By integrating these two separate activities, we are now turning *reflective practitioning* into a tangible, thus feasible process. Admittedly, it has been advocated by many theorists for quite some time,[15] but for many hands-on performers it is as yet an abstract, unworkable concept. Figure 8.4 shows how, in daily life, action and reflection may relate to each other in a circular manner, in one continuous *learning loop*.

Based on seven concrete cases, we suggest that moral education within the military has a much greater chance of success if we link a fundamental didactic notion – i.e. the threefold stratification of the integral concept of competence, as aptly depicted by McClelland's Iceberg – logically and concretely to

---

15   The concept of *reflective practice* is credited to Schön (1983), who made a distinction between 'reflection *in* action' and 'reflection *on* action'. The first takes place by critically

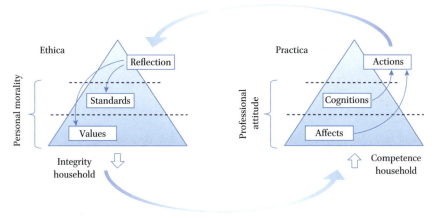

FIGURE 8.4 Reflective practitioning at a glance: The continuous circular relationship between ethical reflection and practical action

the integrity concept, hitherto so vague and elusive for so many. Only in this way, morality may become a natural characteristic of competent professionals.

The purpose of the above considerations is not extrinsic (stay free from negative media attention), but rather intrinsic: contribute to the knowledge of our own, internal Defence household. *Self-knowledge* indeed, because the lack of it eventually might be structurally more devastating to us than occasionally being under enemy fire …

Literature

Angier, T. (2010). *Techné in Aristotle's Ethics: Crafting the moral life*. London: Bloomsbury.

Aristotle (2014). *Nicomachean Ethics* (revised edition). Cambridge: CUP.

Baarle, E.M. van (2018). *Ethics Education in the Military: Fostering Reflective Practice and Moral Competence* (dissertation). Amsterdam: VU University.

Barbalet, J.M. (1997). 'The Jamesian Theory of Action' *The Sociological Review*, 45(1), 102–121.

Baxter, L.A., & Montgomery, B.M. (1996). *Relating: Dialogues and Dialectics*. New York: Guilford Press.

---

examining one's own performance during the act itself. This concerns the immediate, affective, experiential learning in the here and now reality. The second is done by looking back on one's own actions afterwards, by way of a deferred, cognitive analysis. For a more detailed description of this distinction, we refer to Van Doorn & Lingsma, 2019, p. 175 et seq.

Beauchamp, T.L. (2003a). A defense of the common morality. *Kennedy Institute of Ethics Journal, 13*(3), 259–274.

Beauchamp, T.L. (2003b). The nature of applied ethics. In: R.G. Frey, C.H. Wellman (ed.), *A companion to applied ethics* (pp. 1–16). Malden: Blackwell Publishers.

Colaiaco, J.A. (2013). *Socrates Against Athens: Philosophy on Trial.* London: Routledge.

Coleman, S. (2009). 'The Problems of Duty and Loyalty.' *Journal of Military Ethics, 8*(2), 105–115.

Collier, D., & Adcock, R. (1999). 'Democracy and Dichotomies: A Pragmatic Approach to Choices about Concepts.' *Annual Review of Political Science, 2*(1), 537–565.

Collinson, D. (2014). 'Dichotomies, Dialectics and Dilemmas: New Directions for Critical Leadership Studies?' *Leadership, 10*(1), 36–55.

Cox, D., La Caze, M. & Levine, M. P. (2003). *Integrity and the fragile self.* Aldershot, Hants: Ashgate.

Cox, D., La Caze, M., & Levine, M.P. (2018). *Integrity and the Fragile Self.* London: Routledge.

Davidson, D. (1994). 'Dialectic and Dialogue.' In: G. Preyer, F. Siebelt & A. Ulfig (eds.), *Language, Mind and Epistemology* (pp. 429–437). Dordrecht: Kluwer Academic.

Destrée, P. (2007). 'Aristotle on the Causes of Akrasia.' In: C. Bobonich & P. Destreé (eds.), *Akrasia in Greek Philosophy: from Socrates to Plotinus* (pp. 139–166). Leiden/ Boston: Brill.

Doorn, G.J. van (2017). 'Organisatiecoaching op basis van de vijf kritieke succesfactoren.' (Organisational coaching based on five critical success factors). *Tijdschrift voor Coaching (TvC), Visieblad voor Professioneel Begeleiden, 13*(4), 81–91.

Doorn, G.J. van (2019). Five critical success factors for coaching: A perspective on the education of reflective practitioners. In: W. Klinkert, M. Bollen, M. Jansen, H. de Jong, E.H. Kramer & L. Vos (eds), *NL-ARMS 2019; Educating Officers – The NLDA and the Bologna Declaration* (pp. 133–154). Berlin/ Heidelberg: Springer.

Doorn, G.J. van (2021). The Quint-essence of Coaching; letter to a colleague. In: M. Sybesma (ed.), *Kleuren van Coaching; een caleidoscopisch perspectief op het vak* (pp. 39–54). Amsterdam: Boom.

Doorn, G.J. van, & Lingsma, M.M. (2013). *Intervisiecoaching: kortdurende begeleiding van lerende groepen* (Coaching peer consultation; short-term guidance of learning groups; 2nd edition). Amsterdam: Boom.

Doorn, G.J. van, & Lingsma, M.M. (2019). *De vijf kritieke succesfactoren voor coaching; kennis en kunde voor de competente coach* (Five critical success factors of coaching; knowledge and skills for competent coaches; 1st edition; 2nd impression). Amsterdam: Boom.

Eccles, J.S., & Wigfield, A. (2002). Motivational beliefs, values, and goals. *Annual Review of Psychology, 53*(1), 109–132.

MORALITY 123

Ennis, R.H. (1987). 'A Taxonomy of Critical Thinking Dispositions and Abilities.' In: J.B. Baron & R.J. Sternberg (eds.), *Teaching Thinking Skills: Theory and Practice* (pp. 9–26). New York: Freeman/Holt & Co.

Evanoff, R.J. (2004). 'Universalist, Relativist, and Constructivist Approaches to Intercultural Ethics.' *International Journal of Intercultural Relations, 28*(5), 439–458.

Fassin, D. (ed.). (2014). *A companion to moral anthropology.* Oxford: Wiley & Sons.

Fesmire, S. (2003). *John Dewey and Moral Imagination: Pragmatism in Ethics.* Bloomington: Indiana University Press.

Gaus, G.F. (2001). What is deontology? Part two: Reasons to act. *The Journal of Value Inquiry, 35*(2), 179–193.

Gedragscode Defensie. https://www.defensie.nl, last consulted: 17 January 2020.

George, F.H., & Johnson, L. (eds.). (1985). *Purposive behaviour and teleological explanations* (Vol. 8). London: Gordon and Breach Science Publishers.

Godecharle, S., Nemery, B., & Dierickx, K. (2014). Heterogeneity in European research integrity guidance: Relying on values or norms? *Journal of Empirical Research on Human Research Ethics, 9*(3), 79–90.

Gordon, J. (1996). 'Dialectic, Dialogue, and Transformation of the Self.' *Philosophy and Rhetoric, 29*(3), 259–278.

Giannopoulou, Z. (2009). 'Objectivizing Protagorean Relativism: The Socratic Underpinnings of Protagoras' Apology in Plato's Theaetetus.' *Ancient Philosophy, 29*(1), 67–88.

Grant, R.W. (2008). *Hypocrisy and Integrity: Machiavelli, Rousseau, and the Ethics of Politics.* Chicago: University of Chicago Press.

Griswold, C.L. (1981). 'Self-knowledge and the ἰδέα of the Soul in Plato's Phaedrus.' *Revue de Métaphysique et de Morale, 86*(4), 477–494.

Griswold Jr., C.L. (2010). *Self-knowledge in Plato's Phaedrus.* Pennsylvania: State University Press.

Hacker-Wright, J. (2010). Virtue ethics without right action: Anscombe, Foot, and contemporary virtue ethics. *The Journal of Value Inquiry, 44*(2), 209–224.

Haidt, J. (2001). 'The Emotional Dog and Its Rational Tail: A Social Intuitionist Approach to Moral Judgment'. *Psychological Review, 108*(4), 814–834.

Hamm, V.M. (1940). 'Literature and Morality.' *Thought: Fordham University Quarterly, 15*(2), 268–280.

Herrick, P. (2015). *Think with Socrates: An Introduction to Critical Thinking.* Oxford: OUP.

Joseph, S. (2006). 'Person-centred Coaching Psychology: A Meta-theoretical Perspective.' *International Coaching Psychology Review, 1*(1), 47–54.

Kessels, J., & Harrison, R. (1998). 'External Consistency: The Key to Success in Management Development Programmes?' *Management Learning, 29*(1), 39–68.

Kessels, J. & Plomp, T. (1999). 'A Systematic and Relational Approach to Obtaining Curriculum Consistency in Corporate Education.' *Journal of Curriculum Studies, 31*(6), 679–709.

Killen, M., Rutland, A., Abrams, D., Mulvey, K.L., & Hitti, A. (2013). 'Development of Intra-and Intergroup Judgments in the Context of Moral and Social-conventional Norms.' *Child Development, 84*(3), 1063–1080.

Koopman, C. (2009). *Pragmatism as Transition: Historicity and Hope in James, Dewey, and Rorty*. New York: Columbia University Press.

Kraiger, K., Ford, J.K., & Salas, E. (1993). 'Application of Cognitive, Skill-based, and Affective Theories of Learning Outcomes to New Methods of Training Evaluation.' *Journal of Applied Psychology, 78*(2), 311–328.

Lönnqvist, J.E., Walkowitz, G., Wichardt, P., Lindeman, M., & Verkasalo, M. (2009). 'The Moderating Effect of Conformism Values on the Relations Between Other Personal Values, Social Norms, Moral Obligation, and Single Altruistic Behaviours.' *British Journal of Social Psychology, 48*(3), 525–546.

Maner, J.K., & Mead, N.L. (2010). 'The Essential Tension Between Leadership and Power: When Leaders Sacrifice Group Goals for the Sake of Self-interest.' *Journal of Personality and Social Psychology, 99*(3), 482–497.

Marton, F., & Booth, S. (2013). *Learning and awareness*. New York: Routledge.

McClelland, D. (1998). Identifying Competencies with Behavioral-event Interviews. *Psychological Science, 9*(5), 331–339.

Milo, R.D. (2014). *Immorality*. Princeton: Princeton University Press.

Moore, C. (2014). 'How to 'Know Thyself' in Plato's Phaedrus.' *Apeiron, 47*(3), 390–418.

Moore, C. (2015). *Socrates and Self-knowledge*. Cambridge: CUP.

Naso, R.C. (2006). 'Immoral Actions in Otherwise Moral Individuals: Interrogating the Structure and Meaning of Moral Hypocrisy.' *Psychoanalytic Psychology, 23*(3), 475–489.

Neher, W., & Sandin, P. (2017). *Communicating ethically: Character, duties, consequences, and relationships*. London: Routledge.

NLDA Staff (2017). *Voorbeeld doet volgen*. Breda: Repro fbd Regional Desk.

Nussbaum, M.C. (1993). 'Non-relative Virtues: An Aristotelian Approach.' In: M.C. Nussbaum & A. Sen (eds.), *The Quality of Life* (pp. 242–269). New York: Oxford University Press.

Nussbaum, M.C. (1996). 'Aristotle on Emotions and Rational Persuasion.' In: A.O. Rorty (ed.), *Essays on Aristotle's Rhetoric* (pp. 303–323). Berkeley: University of California Press.

Onions, C.T. (ed.), Friedrichsen, G.W.S., & Burchfield, R.W. (1966). *The Oxford Dictionary of English Etymology*. Oxford: Clarendon Press.

Pardo, I. (2015). Corruption vs Integrity: Comparative insights on the problematic of legitimacy. In: P. Hardi, P. Heywood & D. Torsello (eds.), *Debates of Corruption and Integrity* (pp. 184–212). London: Palgrave Macmillan.

Pedler, M. (ed.). (2011). *Action Learning in Practice* (4th ed.). Farnham: Gower.

Rogers, C.R. (1947). 'Some Observations on the Organization of Personality.' *American Psychologist, 2*(9), 358–368.

Rokeach, M. (2008). *Understanding Human Values; Individual and Societal.* London: Collier MacMillan Publishers.

Schipper, F. (2016). 'Transparency and Integrity: Contrary Concepts?' In: K. Homan, P. Koslowski & C. Luetge (eds.), *Globalisation and Business Ethics* (pp. 101–119). Farnham, UK: Ashgate.

Schön, D. (1983). *The Reflective Practitioner: How professionals think in action.* New York: Basic Books.

Sheldon, K.M. & Kasser, T. (1995). 'Coherence and Congruence: Two Aspects of Personality Integration.' *Journal of Personality and Social Psychology, 68*(3), 531–543.

Shweder, R.A. (2012). Relativism and universalism. In: D. Fassin (ed.), *A companion to moral anthropology* (pp. 85–102). West Sussex, UK: John Wiley.

Sinek, S. (2009). *Start with Why: How Great Leaders Inspire Everyone to Take Action.* London: Penguin Ltd.

Spencer, L.M. Spencer, S.M. (eds.) (1993). *Competence at Work: Models for Superior Performance.* New York: Wiley & Sons.

Stokes, M.C. (1986). *Plato's Socratic Conversations: Drama and Dialectic in Three Dialogues.* Baltimore, MD: Johns Hopkins University Press.

Storr, L. (2004). 'Leading with Integrity: A Qualitative Research Study.' *Journal of Health Organization and Management, 18*(6), 415–434.

Sverdlik, N., Roccas, S., & Sagiv, L. (2012). 'Morality Across Cultures: A Value Perspective.' In: M. Mikulincer & P.R. Shaver (eds.), *The Social Psychology of Morality: Exploring the Causes of Good and Evil* (pp. 219–236). Washington, D.C.: American Psychological Association.

Vallentyne, P. (1987). 'The Teleological/deontological Distinction.' *The Journal of Value Inquiry, 21*(1), 21–32.

Vauclair, C.M., Wilson, M., & Fischer, R. (2014). 'Cultural Conceptions of Morality: Examining Laypeople's Associations of Moral Character.' *Journal of Moral Education, 43*(1), 54–74.

Veen, P.A.F van, & Sijs, N. van der (1997). *Etymologisch woordenboek* (2nd edition). Utrecht/Antwerpen: Van Dale Lexicografie.

Verweij, D.E.M. (2000). 'Moed: mythe of morele kwaliteit?' *Militaire Spectator, 169*(2), 83–90.

Verweij, D.E.M. (2010). *Geweten onder schot; ethiek en de militaire praktijk.* Amsterdam: Boom.

Vogelgesang, G.R., Leroy, H. & Avolio, B.J. (2013). 'The Mediating Effects of Leader Integrity with Transparency in Communication and Work Engagement/ Performance.' *The Leadership Quarterly, 24*(3), 405–413.

Weber, J., & Gillespie, J. (1998). Differences in ethical beliefs, intentions, and behaviours: The role of beliefs and intentions in ethics research revisited. *Business & Society, 37*(4), 447–467.

Westacott, E. (2015). 'Moral Relativism.' In: J. Feiser & B. Dowden (eds), *Internet Encyclopaedia of Philosophy*. https://www.iep.utm.edu/moral-re/, last consulted: 17 March 2019.

Westermarck, E. (1932). *Ethical Relativity*. London: Kegan Paul, Trench, Trubner & Co.

Westermarck, E. (2017). *Ethical Relativity*. London: Routledge.

Williams, J.T. &, & Shepard, E.H. (1995). *Pooh and the Philosophers: In Which It Is Shown that All of Western Philosophy is Merely a Preamble to Winnie-the-Pooh*. London: Methuen.

Wong, D.B. (2016). 'Moral Relativism.' In: S. Baronett (ed.), *Journey into Philosophy: An Introduction with Classic and Contemporary Readings* (pp. 471–474). London: Routledge.

Worthington, I. (ed.) (2010). *A Companion to Greek Rhetoric*. New York: Wiley & Sons.

Index

Abu Ghraib 8, 24, 46, 52, 95, 97
Adorno 7
Afghanistan ix, 15, 20, 25, 30, 32, 36, 38, 47, 65, 66, 67, 68, 77, 93, 107
Arendt 10, 84, 85, 86, 87, 96
Aristotle 5, 22, 101, 102, 115, 121, 122, 124
Asch 29, 36, 38
Auftragstaktik 94
Augustine 8, 9

Bandura 27, 31, 32, 36, 97
Bosnia 60, 93, 107
Brereton Report 25, 36
bureaucracy 85, 86, 87, 89, 91, 92

chai boy 54
Chora 107
code of conduct 45, 47, 117
Code of Conduct 83, 116
collateral damage 26, 28, 31, 68n.1
compartmentalisation 87
comradeship 3, 27, 50
conscience 28, 83, 85, 95, 105
courage 35, 41, 42, 44, 102, 118

dehumanisation 30
deontology 18
dialogue 5, 10, 21, 33, 34, 35, 100, 106n.5, 108, 109, 117
dilemma ix, 1, 4, 12, 15, 18, 20, 21, 22, 47, 48, 49, 53, 57, 59, 62, 64, 83, 85, 102, 104n.3, 118
drones x, 67, 68, 70, 76, 77, 78
dual loyalty 43, 47, 105

Eichmann 84, 85, 86, 87, 96, 98

Guantanamo Bay 47, 52
guilt 53, 55, 56, 57, 58t.5.1, 59, 61, 62

hazing 24, 28, 46
Heidegger 7, 70
Holocaust 84, 85, 86, 97
Honneth 2, 6, 7, 11, 13, 14

Hueting 41, 41n.1, 42, 42n.2, 43, 44, 46, 47, 50

integrity 42, 46, 48, 49, 104, 104n.3, 108, 110, 114, 115, 119n.14, 120, 121
intention 2, 9, 10
Iraq 8, 24, 46, 52, 65, 95

just culture viii, 12, 25, 33, 34, 35
Just War Tradition 2, 8, 9, 63
Justice 14, 37, 44, 61

Kant 18, 23
Kunduz 47

leadership viii, ix, 35, 45, 61, 87, 94, 108
Lifton 65, 98
loyalty 3, 12, 19, 20, 31, 42, 43, 44, 45, 46, 47, 48, 49, 50, 51, 102, 103, 105, 106, 118

MacIntyre 72, 73, 81
Mali 24, 38, 106
medical ethics 18, 47, 48, 49, 102
Milgram 28, 37
military ethics ii, viii, x, 1, 3, 11, 39, 47, 51n.7, 83, 84, 102
moral competence viii, 12, 15, 20, 21, 22, 39
moral disengagement 5, 12, 24, 25, 26, 27, 28, 29, 31, 32, 33, 35, 40, 59, 62, 83, 92, 97
moral education 100, 111, 113, 114, 119, 120
moral injury ix, 5, 6, 12, 53, 54, 57, 58, 60, 61, 62, 63, 64, 83, 95
moral standards 2, 5, 12, 24, 27, 30, 32, 35, 46, 59, 62, 69, 101, 103, 105, 105n.3, 107
My Lai 24, 40, 41, 46, 50, 51, 52, 90

oath 18, 20, 45, 47
obedience 12, 19, 20, 28, 44, 88, 94, 95, 96, 112

Plato 8, 14, 101, 109, 123, 124, 125
PTSD 12, 54, 56, 57, 58

relativism 30, 103, 106
responsibility x, 2, 10, 12, 28, 29, 45, 62, 83, 84, 85, 86, 87, 88, 90, 92, 93, 94, 95, 96, 103, 117

128   INDEX

safety   19, 34, 36, 42, 45, 50, 51, 58, 59, 73,
        103, 117
Sangin incident   67, 68, 69, 70, 71, 74, 75, 76,
        77, 78, 79, 80, 81
shame   53, 56, 57, 58, 58t.5.1, 59, 61, 62
Shidane Arone   46

technology   12, 69, 70, 72, 75, 75n.5, 76, 77,
        78, 79, 80
Thompson   40, 47, 50, 51, 52, 66

Uruzgan   47, 93, 98, 105
Utilitarianism   16, 17

values   vii, 2, 3, 4, 7, 9, 11, 13, 15, 16, 17, 18,
        19, 20, 21, 24, 25, 27, 30, 32, 35, 44, 45,
        46, 47, 49, 50, 53, 59, 61, 62, 76, 79, 83,
        100n.1, 101, 103, 104, 104f.8.1, 105n.3, 106,
        107, 108, 110, 112, 113, 114, 115, 115n.11, 116,
        117, 118, 119, 120
Vietnam   24, 40, 57, 60, 65, 66, 91, 95, 98
virtue   12, 15, 16, 19, 21, 43, 44, 45, 46, 97, 101,
        102, 115

West Point   49

Zimbardo   39, 99

Printed in the United States
by Baker & Taylor Publisher Services